Quotable Quotes

If the Theory of Wrong is wrong, it proves the Theory, since guys created it.

Wrong is a helium balloon to float the ego above naysayers.

Even a genius is an idiot at home.

If it's worth doing, it's worth doing wrong.

Always buy her the gizmo you want, so there's no need to return it, when it's wrong.

Guys operate their brains in stages, lizard brain, rat brain, human brain (rarely needed).

Wives should continue to give husbands advice, and husbands should continue to follow it— once all other options are exhausted.

Reading directions is like holding a crib sheet in your lap during the big exam—it's cheating.

Sports can be a reason for living—when they don't kill you.

Keep playing sports you are too old to play, before you are too old to play them.

If the warning label threatens death, it's probably fun until you lose consciousness.

We admit it, guys don't get it.

Guys would be stuck like gum on waffle stompers, if we worried all the time about whether we were doing the right thing.

You shift gears in your car. Remember to shift mental gears when you enter the house.

If the cookie crumbles, get out the glue gun.

THE THEORY OF
WRONG

Married Guys Are Wrong and That's OK

Chris,
Best Wishes
Bob Heck
4-12-06

Bob Heck & Jim Thielman

Wrong Tree Ink, LLC
PO Box 309
Richland, Washington 99352
Visit our Web site at www.theoryofwrong.com

Cartoons by Jane Winslow, WinSome Design, Inc.
Cartoon on pg. 113 by Bev Calicoat
Quotations from the website *The Quotations Page*.

Heck, Bob and Jim Thielman

The Theory of Wrong: Married Guys Are Wrong and
    That's OK/Bob Heck & Jim Thielman—1st ed.

ISBN 0-9772426-0-9

1. Marriage—United States—Humor 2. Marriage
    Anecdotes 1. Title

818.602

To Alayne and Pat
who help us forever explore
The Land of Wrong.

Contents

Acknowledgements

We would like to acknowledge many who made this book possible—without implicating them in any imbroglios related to the content or form, for which we take responsibility.

Wrong Jim has been part of a writing group, who offered their insights and encouragement. They include alphabetically, Dan Clark, Georganne O'Connor, Gayle Kaune, Rita Mazur, Dixie Partridge (she read it twice aloud to her husband, hoping he would get it), and Bill Wilkins. In addition, friends read the manuscript and again were encouraging, including Gary Petersen, Stan Kophs, Cary Counts and Dave Payson. Jan Tarantino edited a nearly final version of the book. Jane Winslow of WinSome Design did the cover design, cartoons, and book layout, assisted by Jan Stack-Leuze. Jane (and many others) provided stories for the chapter on wrong gifting.

We would like to recognize actor/writer Matt Smith, whose workshop "How to Put Humor in Your Writing" was the basis of Principle 1 in the Theory of Wrong: Yes, dear, and…(or my wife is always right). Matt did his presentation at the 2003 Conference of the Pacific Northwest Writer's Association.

We also want to thank the community of folks who provided stories about guys demonstrating a lack of empathy or any other male traits. We are still chuckling and we hope our readers are too.

Some scientists made the error of writing books, which we read and used to come up with some of our ideas. We believe we have given credit to these folks throughout the book. The reader would be advised to check the science books before getting into major holiday arguments based on our reading of their work. Remember, we are two wrong guys.

THE THEORY OF WRONG

"I was wrong,
and I admit it
my explanations
don't seem to get it."

—Keb Mo, "I was wrong."
album *Slow Down*, 1998

Introduction: Writing the Wrong

Just because they look like people we've met doesn't mean we've met them. Half the people we meet look like people we know.

Women tend to recognize faces better than men. Had Wrong Bob known this, he would have been ready as he and wife, Alayne, found a place in a church pew. Sunlight waltzed through Tiffany stained glass and tinged stainless organ pipes blue. The choir's united voice echoed off marble and gold.

Then, Alayne said, "We know those people."

The choir hit a clunker. An unexplainable chill gripped Bob's spine. "No, dear, you're mistaken."

"I'm sure we know them!" said Alayne.

"Look," said Bob, "At our age, half the people you meet look like people you know."

Alayne hesitated. She knew Bob was wrong, but if she poked at his ballooning ego, it might burst and douse her dress with ego-goo.

One week later, the same couple approached. After introductions, the husband chuckled and said, "Of course we remember you. We have a picture of you launching a catamaran into surf."

"Oh," said Bob, surprised.

"I snapped it just as the surf jerked your trunks to your knees," said the insensitive husband, laughing loud enough that people stared.

Bob was wrong. If he had known what science is telling us, he would have expected Alayne to be right about this. He would have expected his skill to lie in getting those swim trunks back on at the same time he handled the waves, wind, tiller and lines of his sailboat.

> If she poked at his ballooning ego, it might burst and splatter ego-goo all over her dress.

Seeing his error, Bob created a new theory to explain how husbands could be wrong about people and relationships but still win prizes for knowing trivia, throwing a baseball or drinking beer without swallowing. We call it the Theory of Wrong.

In the remainder of the book we will lead you through wrong principles, wrong gifting, wrong sports and ways to fix things wrong. We will highlight bits of recent scientific thinking on gender. And we will lead you to the joy of wrong. There's good fun and advice along the way from guys who have been there and survived—so far.

We believe men and women can live happily together for moments at a time. Stringing lots of great moments together is the key. *The Theory of Wrong* aims to help you live happily with a mate for many amazing moments and to survive impossible moments with a smile.

Not So Wrong Research Results

- Women's eyes have more cells that are good at figuring out what something is, noticing texture and color. Alayne recognized old acquaintances quickly, because she had a brain designed to do that.

- Men's eyes are good at seeing motion so they can hit a target, launch a catamaran into surf or angle out of a church parking lot and race to breakfast before some have closed their hymnals.

- Men's brain's have two sides—both strong silent types. While one side figures out a map, the other side can suck sports trivia out of the radio. Both sides are working; they just never talk to each other or share what they know. This helps guys launch into adventures without messy thoughts getting in the way. Oh, I forgot to mention that some men have the female pattern brain— so the hunting party doesn't fall off of every cliff.

- Women's brains have two sides—and they talk all the time, sharing and caring, helping each other plan out a safe and happy life. But they might have to turn the map around to figure out where they are going—big deal. Hey, John Wayne, be a good guy and read the map for them.

- Men have twice the saliva as women, good for spitting on opponents and cleaning coffee spills off the carpet—less useful in polishing wives.

Notes from the Cup o' Wrong Café

- There's a right way and a wrong way to do things—pick the one that makes you happy.

- Wrong is a helium balloon to float the ego above naysayers. Right is a lead weight pulling you down where big meanies can poke you in nose.

- Right is like exercise. You know you should, but it hurts. Wrong is like camping on the couch with beer, chips and salsa—your friends all say, you can do this!

- If you can't be right all the time, at least you can sit around the Cup o' Wrong Café and share your troubles with others, who are rooting for you to succeed—because that would mean they have a shot at success too!

- After breakfast or lunch you can head to the Wrong Bar and Grill, where they always welcome wrong guys with open arms, as long as they will tell their tale of woe and laugh about it or let others laugh about it.

- Like tennis, wrong is hard at first but it gets easier and then harder and then easier and harder—so you try golf.

- Live wrong, live long!

The Theory of Wrong

Super Wrong—the low empathy superhero without a license to fly.

I was in Home Depot the other day and overheard a couple arguing over closet storage. The tense husband said, "You won't even listen to my idea!"

His muscular neck bulged as if a mouthful of Doritos had gone down the wrong pipe.

"That's because your idea is so WRONG!" said his wife's stony silence.

He read her mind and grunted like some Frankenstein monster about to strike.

---

* I refers to Wrong Jim; we refers to Wrong Bob and Wrong Jim.

Acting quickly, she mentioned the BIG GAME was about to start and noted how manly he looked with his tongue muscles tensed up, then, cajoled him to trek across the street to Circuit City.

There, hundreds of screens showing the BIG GAME emptied his mind of storage issues and moved him safely into the zone of sports—the rules, the trivia and the relative size of his screen compared to the biggest screen available. He immediately purchased a TV as big as a house and relaxed into poverty.

I let the moment pass without poking an unneeded nose into another's business, but later my conscience nagged me. How could I nap on the couch, seven remotes for a pillow, while even one guy might choose that moment to let a testosterwrong moment do him in?

> How could I nap...
> while even one
> guy might...let a
> testosterwrong
> moment do him in?

The Secret Revealed

I had been freed from such misery when a friend, Bob Heck, opened my eyes like a double espresso.

"The secret is simple," said Bob. "You are wrong and your wife is right. Accept it and live free."

"Really!" I said, like a thirsty kid at the fountain of wrong wisdom.

"You need no longer defend yourself."

"But I can't lie," I said. "Sometimes I am obviously right."

"You don't get it. Admit you are wrong and the worst has happened."

I sat stunned to silence. "No more worst?"

I took a deep breath. You should too—it's unrelated to the theory but deep breaths come at minuscule cost and provide a fabulous return on the investment.

"I get the picture."

"Then, relax. You are wrong and that's ok."

"Wrong is the end of the line. It's a peace treaty ending a war, a tropical beach with no sunburn, a wife with nothing irksome to say…"

> I sat there stunned to silence. "No more worst?"

Superhero of Wrong

We men form our forever brilliant opinions based on TV, the sports page and comic strips. Then, we stick by them like buds in a buddy movie.

We Supermen of right ride our right thoughts through acrobatic maneuvers—like the twist, spin and double flip through leftovers in the fridge. We're oblivious to the smirks of those who see only a guy in a funny cape and tights. Once the guy in tights admits he is out of style and a little chilly, it's ok. Women love men to admit they are idiots.

Whether we plead idiot or idiot savant, guys who admit to wrong can taste freedom. We will try to do better, but we know we will be wrong again and it's ok. Try wrong! Drop the lead halo of right—but not on your toe!

Now I could see how right it was to be wrong. But could I apply the Theory of Wrong to my life? What's more, could I explain to other suffering males that they would be happier in the Land of Wrong? No way! Impossible! It would be preposterous to try changing the mind of some Paul Bunyan who could squash me like a bug in his beard.

Naturally, I decided to try. After all, I'm a guy. I know the impossible merely requires a few spells and an invisibility cape or two. Besides, what's the worst that could happen? (*See table, "The Worst That Could Happen," on next page.*)

Discovering the Land of Wrong

Suffice it to say that whether you are on the left or the right, rich or poor, lame or lithe, a beer guzzler or a wine connoisseur, a Harvard grad or a GED wannabe, in relation to the significant woman in your life, you live in the Land of Wrong.

This means that you get up on the wrong side of the bed, clean up wrong, dress wrong, eat wrong, say goodbye wrong and hello wrong, think wrong, if you think at all, act wrong, move wrong and sit still wrong.

This reminds me of an exchange from Samuel Becket's Waiting for Godot. One guy asks the other what he was doing that caused him some grief. The fellow answers that he wasn't doing anything, to which the first guy replies, "Ah, but it's the way of doing it, if you want to be happy."

This really happened to me. Shopping for groceries, I came home with ground sausage, all purpose thank you cards, and milk. Wife, Pat, pronounced my sausage ground pork, my thank you cards only for baby-showers, and my selected sell-by date on the milk ancient. As Shakespeare put it: Much ado

The Worst That Could Happen

Problem	Solution
You are ridiculed for being wrong.	Hey, so were the last 50 Presidents. Consider running for office.
Your pride is fatally wounded.	That and a broken arm will get you some major pain drugs at the emergency ward of the hospital. Pride is a mere word. A spoken word is nothing but sound waves slapping against the beach of the mind. Let the next wave wash your sandcastle of pride into the surf and forget about it.
None of your macho friends will talk to you.	They never used words when they did talk to you—just grunts and mumbles, which is what they still do—remove your hearing aides or stick beans in there (raw not cooked beans, please!).
You relax for one moment and lose control of your family.	You never had control, baton-brain! They humored you until your job or golf game distracted you and then they did as they pleased.
Your wife no longer respects you.	Learn the difference between respect and love. You respect a drill sergeant's role, you love your wife and she loves you, not that starched commander role you like to wear. Itchy! Itchy!
People laugh at you—not with you.	The angle of laughter is equal to the square root of fear times the probability of joy. Keep smiling like you get the joke and they will come around.
You admit you were wrong and it kills you.	Have you been peaking ahead in the workbook? Stop doing that!

about nothing! She fixed the sausage; I replaced the cards and the milk issue is at the United Nations.

We guys get caught off guard all the time, because we don't understand how doing nothing the wrong way could get us in trouble. Do you want to be right? First, define nothing to a wife's satisfaction. Guys don't notice half the nothings we are wrong about.

Guys don't notice half the nothings we are wrong about.

But wrong theory only is enriched by such experiences. We realize that men often get sidetracked arguing with wives over nothing. This is fine in winter, when the hot air can heat the house, but the rest of the year it is better to live happy in the Land of Wrong.

Take another example: Wrong Jim was heading on a trip during which Pat would have her birthday. At the last minute, it occurred to him that he could avoid the Land of Wrong by buying Pat flowers and shipping them to a son and daughter-in-law's house, where they planned to spend a few days. This flower thing was new territory for Wrong Jim, but writing a book on wrong can change even one of wrong's champions. A thousand miles away, Jim's daughter-in-law received an unexpected bouquet. Why call ahead to warn a woman that the flowers are not for her?

So, Jim didn't. When he arrived, there were two bouquets, Jim's and his son's. Competing bouquets glared at each other and shouted red-faced: Land of Wrong! Land of Wrong!

Sometimes, right done wrong is like a little asteroid dropped in the ocean. The waves roll on and on. Wife Pat was happy to get flowers but sad she had to leave them behind to travel home. When she dropped them off at her son's office, the women were reminded of how seldom their husbands sent flowers.

If Jim had the empathy of a woman, he might have called or emailed his daughter-in-law to prepare her for the bouquet. He might have realized Pat would enjoy getting the flowers at home for an approaching anniversary. By being a guy, Wrong Jim turned one right into multiple wrongs—then, he smiled to himself, thinking how this might be his personal best score in wrong.

> ...this might be his personal best score in wrong.

The delicacy of these male-female situations escapes most guys—including Jim's brother, Dan. Early in Dan's marriage to Christine, he thought of how much fun they had doing winter sports in mountains, where long johns are required. Wouldn't it be great, if they had matching red union suits? Unfortunately, when he gave his wife her Christmas present, he didn't realize that petite would no longer fit. Too big a size would have been insulting, too small was an embarrassing reminder she was losing the Battle of the Bulge. Also, she didn't know her guy had imagined them together on romantic adventures or even that he had a matching union suit. For Christine, the gift was a red flag that seemed to shout, "You're fat!" Dan stepped in wrong completely unaware. But that's guys all over. We admit it, guys don't get it.

History of Wrong Dressing

Speaking of clothing, women's fashions change all the time. Women also have outfits—color coordinated ensembles with matching shoes, purses and earrings.

Men lack outfits. A suit is as close as we get to an outfit. If a suit were a true outfit, the shoes, belt and wallet would be blue for the blue suit, gray for the gray suit and chartreuse for the chartreuse suit.

Steve Martin's L.A. Story captures a scene where the wife is worried about her outfit and changes over and over before meeting him at the curb in yet another outfit. Guys couldn't do this. They don't have the patience or the outfits.

When men walk into a closet full of clothes, they come out wearing the wrong stuff at least half the time no matter what's in the closet. That's why men's clothing is simple, conservative and pretty much unchanging.

In an eon or two, men's fashions changed from the gown look of Jesus' time to tights that Shakespeare wore and finally to our modern day pants and shorts. Not only do men's fashions evolve slowly, the steps in evolution are all still visible— the flowing robe look is still the in thing in the Middle East and parts of Africa, and male joggers sometimes wear tights that would have blended well into Elizabethan England.

The purpose of this simplicity is so that men will not have to think about what to wear, which would only lead to extreme brain strain and no noticeable improvement in fashion. When it comes to clothes, men see wrong and fail to notice details. Six shades of tan on one body look good to us.

> Six shades of tan on one body look good to us.

Graphophobia Deconstructed

Certain male subgroups carry the bad dressing theme to extremes. Most notable are selected engineers.

Subsets of these brilliant people are known for mixing plaid shirts with different plaid or check pants. The scientific explanation for this is graphophobia—the fear of being caught without graph paper.

One simply removes shirt or pants and sketches the idea in the quadrants created by the plaid fabric. The fact that you seldom see this happening makes it no less true that graphophobia exists—the phobia leads these men to carry loads of graph paper with them along with pencils, pens, calculators and computers of all kinds. Although they seldom if ever use their backup clothing for graphics, it's there if they need it—meanwhile, they can tell the doctor exactly where it hurts: "Four squares down from the pocket point, Doc."

Men and Women Think Differently

Well duh! And it isn't something you can do anything about in your lifetime, which we assume is where your interest lies.

Politically, men inhabit a broad range of positions from conservative to liberal. This makes us no less wrong in our beliefs. Ask a significant woman and you will find out how wrong you are. You are wrong because you tend to see things in terms of black and white or shades of gray.

Women see things in color and five or six dimensions with music and lights swirling through their thoughts and ineffable emotional content soaking like spilled perfume through the sponge of their reality. As a result, you are always a few dimensions behind and below to the left or right of where you ought to be and you smell funny.

Perhaps you've seen the item floating around the Internet showing a man and woman from an engineering standpoint.

The man is pictured as a metal box with a single on/off toggle switch. The woman is a similar box with switches, lights and knobs suggesting orders of magnitude more complexity—and explaining why men can't understand women and women keep thinking there must be more to a guy than that. Sorry ladies.

Men also love logic (and can get very emotional about it). Unfortunately, reality moved beyond logic at the time of the extinction of the dinosaurs, whose famed philosopher, Socrates Triceratops, had just developed a rock solid syllogism that proved the Triceratops would live forever.

So, when it comes to arguments with women, men tend to be these linear, logical, lost beings floating like dust through the multidimensional reality inhabited by the wife. The solution: give up trying to be right. Embrace the wrong, that's where the gold is for a guy.

What if the Theory of Wrong is Wrong?

It's a legitimate question. Suppose like medical research we change our theory based on new information and decide that men are always right. We figure out that the things men do only seem stupid or wrong, but if viewed from a distance—say one universe right or left of this-one, men are always brilliant about relationships. Why would anyone want to follow a theory that is wrong?

Or, what if our advice is like the food pyramid, or is it now the food trapezoid or geometric dome? Advice changes, but our advice has one eternal core of absolute truth (drum roll please).

If the Theory of Wrong is wrong, it proves the Theory, since guys created it. Right or wrong, we think our theory is solid and exactly what you would expect wrong guys to come up with.

That's why the Theory of Wrong is so wonderful and beckons guys like some unattainable goal—the hole in one, the wife we understand or the undiscovered Northwest Passage.

One more reason you should believe us and our theory is that the Northwest Passage is about to open in the Canadian Territory of Nunavut due to global warming. The early explorers looked in the wrong place and forgot to bring their diesel-powered icebreakers.

We learned this like we learn everything, while drinking and chowing down with a smarter and richer brother-in-law, who traveled there and should know, even if he is a guy.

Of course, we forgot to tell you that on the trip he was stopped for three hours by Canadian Customs and nearly arrested as a terrorist. Either that or he was so charming, they wanted to keep him around awhile. We suspect that was the issue.

In either case, he was put through many hoops, partly because when asked which part of Canada he would be seeing he said, "None of it." He meant Nunavut and they probably knew what he meant, but if his wife had been with him, she would have added a few details to be sure the official knew he wasn't trying to be snide.

Did I mention this brother-in-law is a retired pathologist? He is highly knowledgeable, but his work didn't require him to develop an easy going bedside manner, since his "patients" were approached as tissue slides or dead bodies.

> Embrace wrong, that's where the gold is for a guy.

Research tells us that women tend to be better at reading emotions written on our faces. It wouldn't surprise me to learn that the female custom's official read annoyance and impatience on my broth-er-in-law's face and decided to let him sweat awhile.

The official sent him to another line, where he waited while the Hudson Bay Company sheered a flock of sheep, processed the wool and made some blankets.

He made it to Nunavut, and now he knows what Lewis and Clark didn't know. If they had crossed the continent further north and a few hundred years later, they could have made some polar bears a nice meal. They also would have discovered the long sought Northwest Passage.

It just goes to show how important timing is and how wrong guys can be—even when they are as famous as Lewis and Clark and full of pemmican, which is a Native American food that tastes like Spam mixed with ants and pine needles and is said to be very nutritious. A guy invented it.

Notes from the Cup o' Wrong Café

SUPER
Extra Strong
Jet-Black Coffee

- If you've only got one life to live, why not live it wrong? If you have more than one life to live, relax. You can fix things next time.

- It bears repeating: If the Theory of Wrong is wrong it proves the Theory, since guys created it.

- Men are from Montana, women are from New York and children are from Iowa—as long as they go back where they came from by tonight, I don't see a problem.

- If the shoes fit, who cares if they match?

- If the shoes don't fit and the pants don't fit, maybe it's time to stop wearing the stuff you bought in junior high.

- If your wife lets go of a plastic bag while she cuts the raw chicken, put a snack in there and run before she can shout, "Salmonella!"

- The nice thing about this theory is how it welcomes all men with open arms, almost as if it were the woman of their dreams—a gorgeous bimbo with excellent helping skills, a dead mother-in-law, a certificate from the Culinary Institute of America, a degree in erogenous massage, a rich uncle about to leave her a fortune, and a high paying job until the uncle thing comes through. Nice huh?

Not So Wrong Research Results

1. Life Priorities: Guys are more likely to chase status at the expense of family—wrong but how else will you get a shinny shelf of trophies for the kids to dust?

2. People vs. Systems: Job-interest inventories show women are more interested in people-jobs and men in systems-jobs. She teaches the world to sing, he sings to himself as he designs the sewer system.

3. Risk: Men are more reckless in 14 of 16 measures of risk-taking. This can be positive as in exploring new ideas or negative as chronicled in the Darwin Awards. She might take a chance with thin icing on cake, while he skates on thin ice.

4. Spatial abilities: Men are better, in general, at rotating a 3-D image mentally. He can imagine Brittany Spears turned upside down.

5. Math differences: In general, women score better at calculation, men at word problems and mathematical reasoning. He tells a good story problem, while she figures out if it adds up.

6. Variability: At the extremes of the bell-shaped curve there is more variability in men—that is, more idiots and geniuses. So, women can be idiots, but more men take to it naturally—especially after a few beers.

7. Women tend to be better at some verbal tests and manual dexterity, men at hitting targets. He can toss the bean bag; she can sort beans and say when he's full of them.

Except for the silliness and item 7, taken from Steven Pinker's debate with Elizabeth Spelke at Harvard. Search Google.

Wrong Principles

♪ All around the knitting wife
went hubby's puffed up ego!
His wife needled him in fun
POP! goes his ego!

If we are going to do the wrong thing right, we need some principles. Facts are fine, research discoveries are first-rate, truth is ideal but principles allow us to ignore all that hard stuff and write a book where we appear to know what we are talking about without actually doing any thinking, which in our view would be wrong or at least difficult.

I wonder how many principles we should dream up. One would be unforgettable, three memorable, seven hard to recall. I think we should have ten like the Ten Commandments, so people can conveniently forget the one that applies at any particular moment.

We've already introduced some of the principles more or less accidentally. Now let's wrestle some truth out of them using the brute force brain module guys share with tigers.

The Wrong Principles

1. Yes, dear, and...
   (or my wife is always right).

2. If it's worth doing, it's worth doing wrong.

3. Testosterwrong trumps happiness if you let it.

4. Men see, think, touch, taste, feel and act wrong.

5. It's ok to be wrong.

6. You can only be wrong, not more wrong.

7. Only the wrong can learn right.

8. Learn the Wrong and it will set you free.

9. Wrong feels right, which is the joy of wrong.

10. Live wrong, live long.

What do these principles mean? I don't know. But without principles, you can't have a self-help book and without a self-help book, I would have to get a real job. So, let's see if we can make something inspiring or at least as rousing as a thumb tack on a chair seat out of our 10 principles.

Principle 1
Yes dear and...(or my wife is always right).

Let's say your wife says it's Tuesday and you know it's Wednesday. She is clearly, inescapably wrong. Nevertheless, the Theory of Wrong tells guys not to get sucked down the disposal drain trap of right.

Pause a moment. Give yourself time to quiet the voice of Right, and his two-year old buddy Gotcha, so you can listen. We know listening is virgin territory. The last time we listened, Elvis was crooning about hound dogs, but hey buddy, go ahead and give it a try.

Wrong Theory says that in any interaction with a mate, a guy should do what any self-respecting improvisational theater pro would do. If you've watched them, you know that these guys risk the death of ego day after day as they stand in front of live audiences with no script and no net. They literally live at their wits' end.

Since public speaking is dreaded more than death by many, improvisational theater is akin to suicide—or it would be without strict rules. The Golden Rule is that if your partner speaks, you agree and add to it. Then, she agrees and adds to that. The name of this rule is "Yes and...." It is extremely powerful, so don't be blown away the first time you use it.

Let's look at an example. If Jane says, "Oh, look it's started raining" and Joe says, "No, that's not rain" or "No it's sunny" it kills the skit dead. There's no place to go—game over.

Wild things happen in these skits, so what follows from "It's started raining" can be unexpected, even outlandish, but it can't change the rain to sun. That's the rules, like football, where you can't score a field goal on the kickoff.

Following the rules, Joe could respond to Jane by saying, "Yes and it's a warm rain. I'm stripping down to my swimsuit and jumping in the surf."

"Look out for sharks," Jane might say.

"There's one. I'd better get my shark shooter!" Joe says… and so on.

Let's say you and your wife are going to dinner and the Mother Hen in her head says, "You'd better bring a coat," you may want to respond, "I'm tough, cold doesn't bother me" or "You call this cold? This is tropical."

Playing the "Yes and…" game you could say any of the following when she says "bring a coat":

"Yes and an umbrella in case it rains."

"Yes and my gloves too."

"Yes and I'll warm up the car."

"Yes and the Coleman Stove, in case we get stranded."

"Yes and the down comforter."

The last two comments could get you in the same hot

Actor/writer Matt Smith taught this rule at a Pacific Northwest Writers Association conference in Seattle in 2003. This application is our own.

water you were heading for. "Yes and a blow torch to thaw my fingers" is definitely sarcasm.

So, practice playing along via the phrase "Yes and…." You might have to bite your tongue and swallow some blood now and then or say the phrase "yes and…" over and over like a mantra to empty your mind of the smart-aleck invective crowding up to the edge of the playing field like rabid fans. Remind those guys they are spectators. You are the coach/player and this is your stadium. Own it.

> Half of marriage is ninety percent agreement.

To paraphrase Yogi Berra, "Half of marriage is ninety percent agreement."

Now that you've got this down, you can apply the energy you saved to the really big stuff—like which one of you is going to get up in your jammies, check the deadbolt on the front door and switch off the lights. Don't forget to leave your slippers where you can trip over them later in the night. Yes, and I almost forgot…pleasant dreams.

Principle 2
If it's worth doing, it's worth doing wrong.

The point is that we guys would be stuck like gum on waffle stompers, if we worried all the time whether we were doing the right thing. The reason guys exist is because the world needs people who confidently march into the mouth of the beast without qualms or toothpaste.

Sometimes, we lose a few male explorers, but often they find a way out of the whale, like Jonah, even though by rights they should be dead. Come to think of it, Jonah is dead, but the whale didn't kill him thanks to (pick one) a) Yahweh's plan, b) the power of positive thinking or c) the whale was vegetarian and renting rooms in his belly.

Let's say the enemy isn't a beast, but a new idea. Some guys will keep trying until they invent a light bulb, even though they fail over and over and finally discover that Edison already did that in his sleep.

> Doing things wrong over and over until something works is what men are here for...

Doing things wrong over and over until something works is what men are here for, so please enjoy your mistakes and fail forward. There are plenty of guys behind you willing to fail forward a few thousand more times, until the ball crosses a goal line, swishes a net, or shatters the neighbor's picture window for an indisputable though high-priced home run.

It's part of the beauty of guys that we never give up. Sometimes this can be annoying to women. We once had our carpets cleaned on the coldest day of the year and the guy refused to be beaten by a little weather. He was smiling. After all, he was in the Carpet-Cleaning Super Bowl!

His hoses froze repeatedly. It took three times longer than normal, but he finished against all odds, while "Gonna Fly Now," the theme to Rocky, blared on his truck radio. However, as he worked, the door stood open. His frozen hoses marred all the corners in the house, and we are still paying off the heating bill under an installment plan. As a guy, I was energized by his performance—realizing that I too could accomplish anything, if I set my mind to it—like never getting hired to do household chores for my wife.

Hey, if a guy were flexible, he wouldn't be a guy. Costs would fall, the economy might collapse and Champagne would never be squirted over players and announcers. Hollywood would have to think of a new plot for action movies. The effort would overheat the industry's brainpower resulting in a massive BRAINBURST that would darken the skies and freeze the earth. Then, our hero would ride into town and John Wayne the guys that are left. "Fellas," he'll drawl, "We gotta stop thinking if we wantta save the planet."

Next, Hollywood would make yet one more blockbuster movie called BRAINBURST with the same old plot. It's no use messing with guys.

Principle 3
Testosterwrong trumps happiness, if you let it.

Face it, testosterone is great stuff and gives guys more gusto than we know what to do with. That's why we put ourselves on treadmills—trying to burn enough energy so we don't spontaneously combust. But superhuman guy-power doesn't help us back away from fights with anyone, even the girl of our dreams.

If we insist on winning the game of life, that's great. If we think we can win the game of love, we are wrong. There's no end zone, just a series of erogenous zones. Saying that the scoring is complex is like saying the universe is big. We can bang our heads against a wall

> Saying the scoring is complex is like saying the universe is big.

...you can't smash-mouth a relationship...

until it caves, but we can't smash-mouth a love relationship. Best bite our tongues and then kiss the testosterwrong-powered talk goodbye—at least until we get to the next battle on the field or in the conference room where toughness pays.

Oddly, science is now telling us that low-to-moderate testosterone levels are what provide men with the ability to perform well on tasks that require solving problems.

A little testosterwrong goes a long way. Actually, it doesn't make too much difference (except to baseball and Congress and possibly our long-term health) if we add more testosterone as adults. It makes a big difference if we increase the amount in the womb. Scientists in their lonely labs have injected pregnant rats with testosterone and produced female rats that like tackle football—or something like that.

Guys can increase levels of testosterone by winning a game or acting aggressively. Aggression increases testosterwrong in guys, but testosterone pills don't necessarily increase aggression unless we are already punching our own angry-button.

Very high levels of testosterone way back in the womb can lead much later to work as a courtroom attorney, commodities broker or race car driver—people who feel very comfortable in a high-risk environment.

High testosterwrong in the womb can also lead to extreme behaviors—like cutting your broker's desk apart with a chainsaw when he loses your money. Here's a tip: a screwdriver will dismantle most modular office furniture.

Principle 4
Men see, think, touch, taste, feel and act wrong.

Take for example, spitting. Science has proved that men produce twice as much saliva as women, which enables them to chew tobacco and spit shine their shoes, preferably not at the same time. Many women consider spitting a filthy habit, which is why spittoons are not as popular as they once were.

Several times at work, I've heard guys say, "I don't want to get into a spitting contest with them." They say this because they've been in spitting contests and recall that while the victories were sweet, the laundry bill was horrific.

Women consider spitting contests fundamentally wrong and they are right, but it doesn't solve the main issue of what to do with all that extra saliva. My suggestion is that, while you are biting your tongue to keep from vocalizing your wrong thinking, you also swallow now and then.

Even if you can solve the spitting issue, your thinking, acting, touching, tasting and so forth will still be wrong.

My wife is currently spending an entire week getting a zillion things ready to take on a trip to a lake cabin. I've done one thing related to the trip thus far—I packed some wine and beer to take along.

She's done half the things she can think of and is ready to launch into the next half and the half after that. When we finally climb into the car in

Even if you can solve the spitting issue, your thinking, acting, touching, tasting and so forth will still be wrong.

a couple days to begin the trip, she will fall into her seat and sleep so she can begin the half a zillion things that need to be done when we arrive.

Is there a time measurement for less than zero?

When she's not getting ready to go, she's wondering how I can sit at my desk writing this stuff, while she is busy trying not to forget all the things we will need.

Once we arrive, I will not have half the things I wish I had, because I spent very little time (is there a time measurement for less than zero?) preparing for the trip.

But that's ok. I'm a guy. If I had brought more clothes, they would be the same as the clothes I will bring, because all my clothes are the same.

Sure I might be sleeping in my jeans and swimming in my underwear, but the bed won't mind. I'm a little worried that the neighbors might notice the underwear as bathing suit idea—so I'm ending this to get my swimsuit right now.

Principle 5
It's ok to be wrong.

This is one of my favorite principles. It gets us away from wishing we were always right and into the hot tub warmth of the whole Theory of Wrong.

Wrong is ok. In fact, it's better than ok, but let's not gloat, or we might get a penalty for celebrating like a college football player who has just scored a touchdown.

The thing is you can't help it that your brain is different from your wife's. You can't help it that your ability to develop and maintain a relationship is that of a kindergartener and hers is the equivalent of a postdoctoral degree.

Ok, don't let me pressure you. Maybe you aren't quite in kindergarten yet. You're a guy. It's ok for you to be wrong. We wouldn't have it any other way. So, relax and enjoy life in the wrong lane on the wrong road to the right place—happiness.

Our friend science really is helping us here. Brain researchers have figured out that women have more white matter and men have more gray matter or maybe the other way around.

The thing is, women have their thinking, feeling, sensing and intuiting abilities scattered throughout their brains like it was some multistory townhouse and they were keeping something useful in every room. Not only that, the townhouse has an intercom system so the different rooms can discuss things with each other whenever they want.

Men's brains are like an easy chair with a remote control in the same townhouse. A man's brain lives life in that comfy chair and wonders why the wife won't let him rent out some of the spare rooms upstairs.

> Men's brains are like an easy chair with a remote control...

Men can be incredible scientists or thinkers because they are so focused. But step beyond their area of expertise and an Einstein becomes just another wrong guy.

But now we know it's ok to be wrong. We are ready to enjoy life. If right is ok and wrong is ok, then I guess I'm ok. I'm feeling tiptop already.

Principle 6
You can only be wrong, not more wrong.

Herein is salvation. You bite the bullet and admit you are wrong and that's it. Game over. Shake hands with your opponent and go back to your corners waiting for the next round. When the bell rings, when she turns you around with a whisper, nudge or verbal low blow over your next stupid move, it signals a new round.

> All of life is only moments. Multiply the ones where you connect with your spouse with laughter...

Meanwhile, you needn't live in fear of being wrong again and again. All of life is only moments. Multiply the ones where you connect with your spouse with laughter over how wrong you are this time. Soon you will be enjoying life instead of defending yourself in the court of right and wrong. You will smell the flowers more often than the muck that helped them blossom.

True, this isn't always easy for guys to do. One problem is those verbal blows women seem able to deliver so effortlessly. Most guys, TV announcers excluded, aren't as gifted as women at chat. It's a trade-off men make for having all that power at map reading and motion detection. Your right brain is amazing at spear throwing, but it doesn't help you score points when armed with witty repartee instead of steel.

We theorize that at least some male on female violence results when a woman says something true and right and slightly belittling to a guy, who knows how to deliver a potent message physically but not verbally.

Guys, who admit they are wrong, benefit. We don't need to strain our brains manufacturing excuses. Instead of striking out, we can smile and hug the woman who agreed to share our life and critique our domestic skills for one low price—ok, maybe it takes a moment to switch from seething to smiling, but we have internalized the secret of wrong: You can only be wrong, not more wrong.

For example, you are wrong for leaving the milk bottle on the counter instead of putting it back in the refrigerator. If your wife complains, and you fix the problem by putting it in the refrigerator on the wrong shelf, you are wrong again—but not more wrong. These are separate incidents. Besides, a guy has to have some principles and one of ours is that you can't be more wrong.

Moreover, when you finally put the milk away four hours late, it was no longer milk but bad yogurt. Things were definitely growing in there. What is it about you and milk anyway? You spilled it as a child, left it out as an adult and put it away when it had begun to smell like sweaty sneakers. Even so, we are with you buddy. We are rooting for you and so is your wife. She wants you to be happy as long as she is happy too.

...they can smile and hug the woman who agreed to share their life and critique their domestic skills...

The way to achieve happiness is to move on from wrong to wrong like crossing shark infested waters on rock solid stepping stones. Each stepping stone is a principle in the theory of wrong. Don't ask us how we built them in the ocean. Maybe they are turtles or something—just be happy they are there for you.

By the way, it is possible that our logic is flawed here and there. We might be wrong. But we are not going to let that bother us and you shouldn't let it bother you. The world is big enough to handle a few contradictions, so our theory has to be equally accommodating.

As Emerson said, "A foolish consistency is the hobgoblin of little minds." Consistency also makes candy bars boring, which is why they put almonds in there.

Principle 7
Only the wrong can learn right.

...two inches in the little universe might measure two million miles in the big universe—good for guys who feel cheated in the manhood department.

The whole idea behind learning stuff is that you don't know all the answers. Once you know the answers you freeze your brain. But unlike ice, your brain doesn't thaw every spring.

William James pointed out that the ideas gained by men before they are twenty-five are practically the only ideas they will ever have. It's hard to have a new idea after a certain age and harder still to change old ideas we know are right.

Meanwhile, physicists are challenging old ideas and telling us that there are eleven dimensions not three plus time. Brian Green says in his book The Fabric of the Cosmos that small and large spaces tucked inside our world and invisible to us might exist following the same rules or laws.

The small universe could be the inverse of the large universe. This means that something that measures two inches in the little universe might measure two million miles in the big universe—good for guys who feel cheated in the manhood department. Sometimes new ideas can cheer a guy up.

Principle 8
Learn the wrong and it will set you free.

I like the sound of this principle. Sort of like butterflies are free and know the truth and the truth will announce in a loud voice that your fly is unzipped—a good thing although you might ask the truth to tone it down a bit.

The idea is that if you follow our wrong principles you can enjoy collecting incidents where you said, did or lived wrong but survived and flourished. You can be set free of the guilt that often weighs on those who are wrong.

Meanwhile, where you were defensive about wrong in the past, or wondered if someone else was keeping track and badgering you, now you approach being wrong with joy. You gather a collection of wrongs and store them with your stamp collection, next to your golf tee collection and left of your bobblehead collection.

This solves the problem mentioned earlier that men were put here for a reason but no one tells us what it is. Your wrong collection offers you endless enjoyment, and unlike Lego's, you keep getting more pieces everyday.

...men were put here for a reason but no one tells us what it is.

Principle 9
Wrong feels right—which is the joy of wrong.

You have an excuse now for being wrong.

Do we need to explain this? Sure you were once all smiles when your parental units said 'right' as they whipped through the flash cards of animals, spelling-bee favorites or second-order-polynomial equations—whatever those are.

Now you are a man (or a woman trying to understand a man) and it's been awhile since anyone has smiled at you and said, "Gee whiz, you sure are right about that, Hector."

This is partly because your name isn't Hector and partly because she isn't there when you win that game of solitaire, so you have to cheer for yourself. But she will be there when you do the next wrong thing, since by definition a guy is right until his wife finds the firstborn's birthday cake is missing a layer.

In this case, having learned our Theory of Wrong you admit your mistake, exhaling defensiveness and inhaling the joy that comes from being full of burgled birthday cake.

Principle 10
Live wrong, live long.

We have no data to back this up. But talk to any old guy and you will probably hear something like I heard from my father-in-law: "I'm master of the house, one word from me and she does as she pleases."

Or from the famous Anonymous: Compromise—an amiable arrangement between a husband and a wife whereby they agree to let her have her own way; Marital Freedom—the liberty that allows a husband to do exactly as his wife pleases. Anonymous also came up with the famous universal answer of the happy husband to any query from a wife, namely, "Yes, Dear," or "Yes, Dear, and…" our first principle of wrong.

Those who have lived awhile know better than to take life too seriously, unless they are in politics, banking or plumbing. The rest of us out here aiming to attain a triple digit age have to learn to let things go.

I was on the golf course just last week and one member of the group behind us caught up with us all hot and bothered and said, "Please, please put the flag in straight! The last couple times it's been slanted."

…one word from me and she does as she pleases…

Now, I hate to judge another, but that man may need some stress relief that golf isn't providing. Of course, I must admit that on the next hole my partner had to remind me not to stress out over a missed putt. "Look around you," he said, "You're in a beautiful location, next to a beautiful river on a perfect day. Relax."

I looked at him like he was from some other planet. What was this guy thinking? If I had made that putt…come to think of it, it wouldn't have mattered. I took a couple deep breaths, pushed the reset button on my heart and was happy to feel the blood coursing once again through my veins—plus a tiny trickle clearing cobwebs from the two wrong sides of my brain.

Just "Dude" it! Dope-amine in Action! Fume, focus, function and (let her) fix it.

If you are a guy, you don't let things stand in the way of completing a task. You've read the "Take a letter to Garcia" tale where a guy moves heaven and earth to take an item, technically called a letter, to a guy code-named Garcia. A few lives were lost along the way, but the letter got through and Garcia finally paid the old laundry bill he had neglected.

Guys favorite games, stories and movies feature males overcoming incredible odds without complaint or liability insurance. Dopamine, testosterone, adrenaline and a few more chemicals help. But it's attitude that is critical and the attitude that works best is to fume first and fast. But fuming without focus is useless.

Winners quickly transfer that fuming energy into total focus on getting the task done no matter the cost. They put mind and body in gear and function. Right now! They charge forth with blinders fixed so they can't see the collateral damage they are creating. In the movies, guys never have to pay the damages, or they are so rich by the end of the movie that we figure it wouldn't matter. They break stuff, snuff out villain's lives and move on.

But real life has this annoying thing called consequences. Owners of ruined property and relatives of villains sue the hero and collect damages. Sometimes a replacement for the Ming vase broken over the villain's head isn't available—even on Ebay.

That's why tough guys should have a mate with unlimited calling minutes on her cell phone. She can schedule court appearances, deal with insurance agents, lawyers, doctors and the media—getting our hero back in the game quickly.

The Joy of Wrong

Be back in 2 weeks to help honey... MAX!

This is not a book about how bad men are. After all, at their last physicals, Wrong Bob and Wrong Jim both had major parts appropriate to men, including beards, nose hairs and giant egos. It hurts each time the wives try to box our egos up and sell them as scratch-and-dent items on eBay. We make fun of males only because laughing at ourselves keeps us from crying—a very un-male thing to do.

We would not have put together this book, if we didn't think it would help guys (or if you are a woman, the guy close to you munching chips in your ear as you watch *Antiques Road Show*, while reading this and noting tomorrow's meeting agenda or dinner menu in the margin). Face it. We are all drowning in the same pickle barrel—only we hope to show you a way out of the barrel and into a vacuum-packed jar. Freshness, sparkle and shine are everything to a guy—at least that's what my wife keeps hoping in spite of the evidence.

Nor do we think you guys out there should lie down like a socialized small dog and expose your jugular to the boss at work, coworkers or the mountain lion stalking as you jog through the woods. Toughness has its place—for instance, in pistons, cable bridges and Vibram-sole shoes. Wait a minute. Vibram soles are soft and tough! How about that! Maybe men should be off the scale on flexible toughness. Anyway, don't stop being a guy just because you are wrong.

Also, we all know folks that love the give and take of battle. Aunt Addie and Uncle Clarence were like that. They tussled from kitchen to bedroom and back. Every time they came to visit they had stories about a new way to get lost and which one turned the wrong way this time.

"You said to turn and I turned."

"I said no such thing. Besides I meant turn the other way."

The names attached to the dialogue are interchangeable. It was the battle that was eternal and true and good.

Expecting to be wrong can be relaxing.

Addie always said with a twinkle in her eye and a vodka and ice in her hand that she loved to fight because it was so much fun to make up. (We kept trying to take the vodka away and switch her to low-fat bacon, but it was hard to argue that her habits were killing her at 99.)

Every so often, guys are going to cross the line. Just remember to make it a round trip that eventually gets you back on the right side of your mate. The Theory of Wrong can help. How, you ask?

First, expecting to be wrong rather than right can be relaxing. It's like setting the high jump bar at the height of the low hurdles. You can do this. You can get a beer belly and war wounds over that bar. You go into battle knowing you can win because losing is now winning. Feels good so far, right?

I think it's time for a table to compare the joy of wrong to the joy of cooking. That way we can begin to understand how joy doesn't only belong to gourmet chefs but can be shared by any guy firing up his gas barbeque and burning his fingers on ribs, steaks and chicken.

There is great freedom and joy in being wrong. Why were you golfing when you should have been home figuring out how to make the gizmo talk to the whatchamacallit? You were wrong. No guilt there. It's your natural state. Embrace it.

Some women have proposed a separate hypothesis that there are degrees of wrong. Contrary to the Theory of Wrong's scientific studies at the Cup o' Wrong Café and the Wrong Bar and Grill, a married guy could be more wrong! This idea must be condemned until it can be suppressed, censured and stopped. Otherwise, there goes the joy of wrong—one macho balloon popped and spreading whatever it is in hot air that makes you want to open the windows.

On the other hand, we examined the nature of guys and realized this could work in our favor. If there are degrees of wrong, wrong guys could sponsor a wrong competition. Clearly, some sort of honor would go to the winners.

...we could offer a black belt in wrong...

After five or ten seconds of thought, it occurred to us that we could borrow from the oriental boxing arts like karate and

The Joy of Cooking
Compared to the Joy of Wrong

Joy of Cooking	Joy of Wrong
Gather ingredients.	Snack on ingredients.
Prepare ingredients.	Watch the game while snacking more.
Cook ingredients.	Light the barbeque.
Set the table.	Look for the meal, which is still not cooked and use the opportunity to snack some more while putting the meat on the barbie.
Eat the meal in civilized courses.	Eat the main course on the way to the table.
Clean up.	Set the table while eating leftovers. You can clean up next week.

offer a black belt in wrong. We've carefully outlined what we think the different belts should be as one progresses from slightly wrong to black belt in wrong.

Just remember you can never be more wrong and if you are, you could win a contest. Life is good. Breathe in the wrong; breathe out the bad air of right. Bathe in the joy of wrong.

Since guys are guys, we know once you are aware of the black belt in wrong, you will immediately go into training. Then, you will suffer excruciating pain in your relationship with your spouse to win the Wrong Marathon or Wrong Tournament, or Wrong Grand Tour. Don't!

Why ruin your marriage and your life, for a silly black belt? We know why, because your brain is wired to compete.

Therefore, we propose a simple way to earn your black belt: Enter one of our contests where you tell a true or tall tale of past wrongs committed by you or someone you know. If you are a lucky winner you could win your very own Black Belt in Wrong—assuming our Paris designer stops fooling around and finishes a suitably fashionable creation.

How Bob Got His Black Belt in Wrong

Perhaps an example will help make clear the moves and ducks and dodges that can earn a guy a Black Belt in Wrong. This one involved moving to a new location for the job. This can test the mettle of a spouse. But with a little effort, a guy can raise the bar so high that if the wife gets over it, she moves from suffering martyr to instant sainthood. All she needs to do is handle the entire move and the kids on her own, while he goes off to slay business dragons and earn the respect of his boss.

Wrong Bob knows. He achieved a championship level black belt in wrong by driving the family to their new, but empty, home; simultaneously saying hello to the moving van driver and goodbye to the family. Then, he headed off on a two-week sales trip—leaving wife, Alayne, to handle two children, 150,000 boxes, the furniture and negotiations with the phone company, preschool, newspaper, neighborhood dogs, mail carrier, pharmacy and grocery clerks.

> Ah, the joys of living in the land of wrong.

Ah, the joys of living in the Land of Wrong. Bob returned to find his black belt waiting, although initially it appeared to form a noose hanging from a newly installed block and tackle situated directly over his favorite easy chair—almost as if someone was ready to string him up.

Getting a Black Belt in Wrong

- Mauve Belt—wear this belt in public and you earn it—no heavy lifting required.

- Pink Belt—you forget it's your anniversary and spend the evening at a sports bar before calling to say you'll be a little late—wear pink boldly—you've earned it.

- Yellow Belt—You buy a new sports car without consulting her and park it in front of the neighbor's house for the first month, because you are afraid to tell her the truth—show your true colors!

- Green Belt—You spend a fortune on a men's tour of whatever and then complain that she's wasting money by calling your cell phone everyday to find out where you are—you've got the green!

- Brown Belt—You tell her how great she should feel about your promotion, which requires that she quit her job and move from Santa Barbara to Nome. Then, you pull out a bar napkin to dry her eyes—brown belt baby!

- Black and Blue Belt—she catches you in bed with her best friend and smacks you repeatedly with the new Ping putter you gave yourself for Valentine's Day— earning you the esteemed black and blue belt.

- Black Belt—Since honesty is the best policy, you tell her she is fat, the new dress looks like a Hefty bag, and the coffee tastes like arsenic—come to think of it, that is arsenic.

Enjoy your black belt while you can!

Although Bob couldn't imagine who would want to do that, Alayne could. At this point of his life in the Land of Wrong, Bob was fond of treading from wrong to wrong, as if wrongs were stepping stones. At the end of his sales trip, he stopped at a friend's house in another city. As they were finishing a superb meal at a renowned restaurant (Alayne and the kids were having mac and cheese) the friend casually asked what Bob had gotten Alayne for her birthday. Bob reeled back, like a boxer hit by a left hook. He recovered in time to send flowers that arrived a day late, in time for the furniture to be arranged to properly display the guilt gift.

Wrong Gardening

Life is magical. Lichen and moss can grow on solid granite; gradually converting rock to soil that can feed a tap root in places you wouldn't think a seed could sprout.

Oh, and equally magical—a guy can grow a tomato. Wrong Bob grew them in correct male fashion, as part of a contest with a neighbor, a woman ignorant of modern scientific gardening techniques. Actually, Wrong Bob made his techniques up in the nick of time—just as the contest was underway.

> Life is magical… and equally magical—a guy can grow a tomato.

The contest wasn't fair. Bob had a degree in chemical engineering and knew that the multi-handed molecules in chemical fertilizer would be all over the tomato seeds he planted— cajoling them to grow like crazy.

All Neighbor Joan had going for her was some peat moss, manure, gardening experience, a nursing degree, children who were thriving and half of the agreed on package of tomato seeds.

Then too, Bob was such a whirlwind when it came to growing stuff—like mold on his shower stall—that he once thought he had created life in a test tube. Later, through careful analysis, he deduced that his baloney sandwich made a donation to the test tube, jump starting life in the world's smallest terrarium.

Still, Bob knew as a male he had the upper body strength, eye-hand coordination and powerful right brain to win. Shucks, with his spatial abilities, he would instantly know how to perfectly plant the tomatoes.

Using scientific methods and a charge card, Bob purchased chemical fertilizer at the yard and garden department. Cleverly, he measured out different amounts of fertilizer for each seed from none to a big dollop, noting in his lab notebook how much each seed received. Then he sat back and waited to collect the blue ribbon.

Joan tilled her rich soil, planted the seeds and waited as well.

The results were startling. Bob's tomatoes were all the same size—about 18 ounces. Joan's tomatoes were all at least 24 ounces and her largest tomato weighed in at a hefty 28 ounces. Manure and peat moss beat chemistry and male logic.

> Manure and peat moss beat chemistry and male logic.

In wrong male form, Bob refused to be beaten for good. He entered more contests with Joan and continued to rack up defeat after defeat. He was especially proud of winning the wrong labeling contest, where he grew chard but thought it was spinach. He gave another neighbor an enormous batch of spinach, which she planned to use for the salad portion of a progressive dinner party. Fortunately, she was a woman and tasted the greens finding them surprisingly unlike any spinach she had ever had. She rushed to the grocery store and solved her spinach crisis in the nick of time.

Wrong Suburban

Manure defeated Bob, but Jim's brother Dan found manure for his garden for free. Never look gift manure in the…what's the opposite of mouth? One Friday, late, Dan was finishing a remodeling project when he came upon the freebie. Even though it was late and he was exhausted, he spread a plastic tarp and shoveled the backend of his Suburban full of a load.

Once home, Dan took that brief detour into the house for nourishment which tired him more and led to sleep. The weekend brought a new set of chores and something in the manure had prompted forgetfulness—a foretaste of the underworld where souls drink celestial soda pop and forget they were on earth so they can return without searching out their old address, where they buried Ninja Turtle action figures in the sandbox and hid marbles in the basement.

Meanwhile, biology was at work inside the Suburban. The psycrophilic bacteria thrived and prospered through the cool night. The mesophylic bacteria took over as the temperature rose. When it reached 104 degrees on up, the thermophilic bacteria took over. The result was that all weekend long, families of bacteria were chowing down on carbon, nitrogen and potash and releasing various gases to the surrounding milieu.

Monday morning Dan noticed steam clouding his windows and recalled the free gift. As he opened all the doors, a fragrant fog spewed forth. Clearly, burgeoning life forms were partying down.

The neighbor heard the story and though he had often looked longingly at this Suburban as a future purchase, he quickly went out and bought one from someone else. Meanwhile, months passed. Air fresheners did their work. Still, Dan's daughter cringed every time he offered her a ride.

The garden grew glorious fruits and vegetables making up for the odorific auto in Dan's eyes—eyes which still tear up as he thinks of the story on drives to work and catches a whiff of ammonia working its way out of the upholstery.

Oh, this reminds me of another manure story, showing another side of guys—the need to overdo. Bob's wrong friend, Pete (a pseudonym to protect the guilty), took his utility trailer to get manure. This allowed him to get as much free manure as he could load, which was, of course, a bit more than the trailer could handle. You would think free manure was money, the way guys go after it. Pete piled the trailer high and then drove as far as burning axles and wheels will take you. He stopped to inhale some of the smoke and unloaded half of the load by the side of the road. He proceeded in stop-and-go fashion, until he delivered a couple bags worth of manure to his garden, while helping many weeds attain stunning blooms that year along the roadside.

Notes from the
Cup o' Wrong  Café

To increase joy, listen to your wife when she...

- signals for you to zip up your mouth when you are about to fire a smart comment across the room that you will later regret.

- explains that it isn't the thought that counts, its jewelry that matches her wardrobe.

- tells you not to have another drink, until you prove that you can stand without wobbling.

- suggests you to send flowers to your mother instead of a lifetime supply of fish fertilizer.

- notes that you might want to quit talking to the kids like they were teenagers now that they have teenagers.

- asks you to zip up your pants before you introduce her to your boss at the company picnic.

- explains that you wouldn't show so much butt crack fixing the kitchen sink, if you'd reduce the size of your beer belly to a single six-pack.

- tells you where you left your wallet, keys, money, credit cards, glasses, left shoe, watch, wedding ring, pants, and hearing aid…. She should have mentioned the hearing aid first and you might have had a chance of hearing where the other stuff went.

- requests that the discussion of religion and politics be carried on in the privacy of your mind.

- ditto for the comments on that girl's geometry.

Wrong Gifting

You call this a Mother's Day gift??! I call it a budget
item. Flowers would have been fine...*Dear*.

I wonder what would happen if a guy tried to get a gift for
a girl. No, that might work out. What I'm wondering is what
if a guy tried to select a gift for his wife. Gift giving requires a
certain amount of empathy.

Guys operate their brain in stages: lizard brain, rat brain,
human brain (rarely needed). The rule is to never let the lizard
lounge. Use your zero-empathy, fully unconscious lizard brain
stem until it fails you, then fire up your blind-rat brain. When
your wife (called the "farmer's wife" in the nursery rhyme)
figuratively chops off its tail, it's time to pull the breaker and
power up the human or backup-brain. It takes a lot of juice

to turn on the lights in there and hunt for your empathy—be sure to check under the sports page.

In short, the average woman should be better at empathy than the average guy. Now young guys can learn to fake empathy during the courting season. Women would be advised to extend the courting season indefinitely, but it's not really feasible. Sooner or later genetics don't lie and so a guy will eventually give the gift where he doesn't care to send the very best. More than likely, he forgot the occasion as well as the gift, because his lizard was stalking some breakfast spiders.

If it's a general gift giving season, the wife buys all the gifts except the gift for herself. But face facts, a wife expects something for her birthday, Christmas, the anniversary of tying the Gordian knot, and one other date. Hmmm. Wait, I've got it—Valentine's Day.

I should remember Valentine's Day. My son with the Ph.D. had the good sense to get married on Valentine's Day, thus creating an opportunity for the annual twofer gift. How brilliant! He has America's monster media conglomerates

> Beware geeks bearing gifts!
> —Virgil *(with a twist)*

working around the clock from New Year's to February 14 to remind him of his wedding anniversary—all at no cost to him. The only trouble is, as a busy engineer, he pays less attention to media blizzards than polar bears pay to snowflakes, so I'm not sure it will always work.

If you accidentally establish that she produces children that in some ways resemble you (for example, the boy forgets to put down the toilet seat) then throw in Mother's Day too.

She might volunteer that she isn't your mother, but don't fall for that. She is expecting something. I suggest you buy a gift and a backup gift. If the first gift goes over for some reason, which you won't understand, hold back on the backup gift and use it next time. But if the first gift sends her to the bathroom in tears, knock on the door and mention that you were only kidding and the real gift is in the kitchen. Wait until she is comes out and (except for the chefs among us) hope the surroundings remind her to fix dinner, unless the backup gift is a night out at your favorite rib pit. She's vegetarian? Isn't that why rib pits serve bread and coleslaw?

Some men do learn to buy flowers and romantic gifts, but for many men this is treacherous territory. It begins at an early age. Science says in the womb, but it's hard to tell from where I'm standing—a foot taller than my mother.

I do know that over the fourth of July, five children under the age of four were gathered at the family lake cabin. With the Valium pills to calm me, espresso strength coffee to keep me alert, firework explosions to make me deaf and a fridge full of beer, I found the children charming.

The three boys were old enough to compete for engines to toy trains, even though my wife had thoughtfully provided one for each of them. The oldest boy often found reasons why he needed more than one of the engines or all of them. Parents and guardians intervened.

> The joy of giving is a pleasure, especially when you get rid of something you don't want.
> —Frank Butler

Meanwhile, I watched one toddler smile and hand me a gift—a stack of three cups. I smiled at the darling girl, accepted her gift and later gave it back to her. She handed me something else.

She would use the same strategy with the boys, turning their competitive streak upside down with generosity. I assume she will get over this generous streak when it suits her—say when diamonds are involved.

Having just read Simon Baron-Cohen's book, *The Essential Difference*, I felt like I was watching biology in action: Boys competing, a lone girl working the room and networking. It seemed no accident that she was thinking of others and giving gifts. But conclusions based on one incident are unscientific and possibly wrong, which suits me and most guys fine.

I could imagine this girl grown and still giving smiles and presents to those around her. I could imagine the guys grown and still competing at sports or business and being a bit confused about buying gifts for someone invisible when they look in the mirror.

As a result of our hormonal heritage, our active lizard brain, or because our one-track minds can only switch from making to spending money at distant switchyards, we guys often give women the strangest gifts (see table of real gifts men have given): A load of manure for Mothers day; a can opener for Valentine's Day? These gifts are just wrong! Not to mention the ever readily available nothing-at-all. But now you know nothing-at-all transpired because the guy's brain train was running late or searching through Montana for North Dakota.

...our one-track minds can only switch from making to spending money at distant switchyards...

The sad part of this wrong gifting thing is when guys try and fail. The lady that told me about the wrong stapler gift mentioned how hurt her husband was over her lack of enthusiasm for a designer gift he thought she would love. Jim's wrong brother, Dan, had a fun idea in mind when he bought matching union suits for he and his wife to wear for winter sports—but bought the wrong size and raised diet issues that triggered anger. Jim thought he was doing well to finally give his wife flowers, but left her wondering if she would ever get them at home where she could enjoy them for more than a couple days (maybe a grocery-store bouquet).

Often, guys give gifts that are for him as much as for her. Wasn't he planning to eat the vegetables from the fertilized garden, the food cooked in the frying pan, some of the soup the can opener opened? A better gift might have been to cook dinner—even better if he buys the ingredients himself.

Guys buy gifts for themselves and their wives, when they aren't buying gifts for themselves disguised as gifts for her. Jim once gave his wife one of those remote controlled tanks from Radio Shack for Christmas. It was his idea of a joke gift, but she didn't find it as funny as their sons did—or use it as much.

> Guys buy gifts for themselves and their wives, when they aren't buying gifts for themselves disguised as gifts for her.

This had unintended consequences. One son later bought a bunch of clothes for himself and wrapped them as a gift to his wife. You can imagine how his amusement and her disappointment smashed together like tsunami waves.

Actual Gifts from Men to Their Wives

Gift	Occasion	Wrong Thought	What She Wanted
Load of manure	Mother's Day	She likes gardening!	Flowers
Electric range to replace gas range	Christmas	She'll love cooking my meals in this!	Her gas range back and his head in the oven. ˙
Pressure washer	Birthday	Now she can wash the SUV anytime.	Earrings
Duck Decoys	Birthday	I need some duck decoys.	Pheasant under glass
Designer can opener	Valentines Day	It's from MOMA* She'll love it!	Godiva chocolate or a bracelet from MOMA.
Oven Mitts	Christmas	These are so cool!	A hot date with him.
Remote control tank	Christmas	The boys and I can play with this.	Anything else.
Garbage Bags	Birthday	Wow! These new bags are strong and have ties built in!	Kitchen Aid mixer.
Shotgun or Rifle	Christmas	Now we can hunt together, if she will share the gun with me.	A clean shot at him—or a gift as valuable.

*(Museum of Modern Art)

Jim's sister gave her parents elaborate, if inexpensive gifts at Christmas. As a Catholic nun, she took a vow of poverty, so the gifts were of little monetary value, but there were so many of them to be opened one a day over many days. She had put tremendous thoughtfulness into her gifts and the parents appreciated it.

Jim on the other hand, would give them clothes that his wife picked out with excellent taste and so they also looked forward to Jim's gifts, even though they were really from his wife.

For guys, thoughtfulness is something the mind does when engaged in solving a problem. For wives, it is the care that goes into selecting a gift or performing an action that brings people together.

As men grow in age and wealth, they don't grow in wisdom. Take the man who bought his wife an electric range for Christmas and paid a fortune to have workmen install it on Christmas morning and remove the gas range she had cooked with for all of their married lives. She had a small guest list that year—a mere 40 relatives were stopping by for turkey and trimmings. The fact that this would be equivalent to him running a marathon in stiff new shoes didn't occur to him. There was a moment where she wished she still had the gas range with his head securely in the oven.

Wrong Bob and Jim considered creating some rules to help men give the right gift to their wife. The problem is that we so seldom succeed at gift giving. Anyway, we know it's hopeless for many men to change who they are three or four times a year and become skilled at empathy. Instead, we developed rules that describe the wrong way we give gifts (see Rules for Wrong Gifting at the end of this chapter).

How wrong can you be as a gift giver? That's like asking how far is forever. We think a prime example of greatness in wrong gifting was the husband who, having forgotten to get his wife something, wrapped an unopened box of garbage bags and gave her that. He actually was fascinated with garbage and would have been pleased with such a gift himself. Alas, his wife was less impressed. Being empathetic, she noted his interests and later gave him a bright red plastic garbage can for Christmas. She had to curb his enthusiasm or he would have thrown out everything they owned.

> How wrong can you be as a gift giver? That's like asking how far is forever.

Another man, who was thinking ahead, borrowed his wife's wedding rings at Thanksgiving, saying he was taking them in for a cleaning. Instead, the clever man had them melted down and made into new rings that he gave her for Christmas. If he had recorded over the wedding video, he couldn't have done a better job of ripping her heart out.

One way to push the envelope in wrong gifting is in the area of balance. If things are balanced and fair, everyone will be happy. For example, on Mother's Day this year, Wrong Jim bought himself a new car. He bought his wife a jar of jam and a silver bookmark that she actually uses in the novels she is always reading.

The jam turned out to be packaged in a cutsey-jar from hell that only Jim with his superior mechanical and system-izing skill could understand. In fact, it took him an hour to figure out how to get the clasp thingy to camp down on the lid thingy. Then, he tried to hold a seminar to explain how it works to others in the house, but it wasn't well attended.

That left the silver bookmark, which cost $15 to balance the slightly used car, which cost more than a thousand times that. However, the theory of wrong came to Jim's rescue and rather than continuing to argue that these gifts were equitable, Jim bit his tongue so that any further advice came out as, "Bluhhhh!" This helped him survive to tell you about his incredible Mother's Day gift.

> If things are balanced and fair, everyone will be happy.

The stories never cease. One husband wrapped a gift for Christmas, fully aware that the gift was one they had picked out together. He even paid for it with his money, asking no contribution at all from her account. After they used the appliance for a couple months, he snatched it off the counter and wrapped it for Christmas.

We think he deserves a minimum of a green belt and possibly a black belt in wrong for the courage displayed. Did I mention he was, ah…thrifty? To his credit, at least the gift was something they both wanted, instead of the large lump of shiny coal he might have selected on his own.

One of my favorite wrong gifting stories deals with my brother Dave. He ordered a riding lawnmower that happened to arrive the day before Mother's Day. Brilliant brother that Dave is, he tied a bow on the lawnmower and brought wife, Shirley, out to see her Mother's Day gift. Shirley expressed less than ecstatic joy at such a feminine gift from a wrong guy. The sign of how impressed she was came a few weeks later.

"Come on, Dave," she said. "We're going shopping for your Father's Day present."

Dave should have known, but didn't. In the mall, Shirley guided Dave to a jewelry store and let him start looking for a suitable gift. He perused the Rolex watches, diving watches, and solar-powered watches, wondering which item he deserved most. After a time he grew impatient. Shirley was wasting time at another counter rather than helping him reach his decision.

"What's that," Dave asked, as he moseyed over to see what her problem was.

"It's your Father's Day present. Do you like it?"

That's how Dave bought Shirley a lovely new ring for Father's Day.

Telling this story prompted a listener to volunteer a similar one. Only this wife failed to take action at the jewelry store when she ended up with the riding lawnmower. The next year for Mother's Day she got a shiny new shed for her mower.

Rules for Wrong Gifting

1) Always buy her the gizmo you want, so there's no need to return it, when it's wrong.

2) Shopping for her is a good time to stock up on stuff you need anyway but haven't had time to buy.

3) Carbide is cheaper than diamonds and nearly as hard.

4) If it isn't useful, it isn't Christmas.

5) Give her the rose colored glasses first and the riding lawn mower will look better than a bouquet.

6) Be reasonable. If she takes the car on Christmas Eve, she can't expect gifts on Christmas Day.

7) If the thought counts and she likes gardening, consider a load of manure instead of perfume. Remember what Gertrude Stein might have said if someone ever mentioned that her writing stunk, "Aroma is aroma is aroma."

8) If shopping with her in July, make her wrap up any purchases until Christmas.

9) If the gift for her is something you can use, don't wait until Christmas to try it out. Use it when she isn't around and then clean it (this is important) and wrap it for Christmas.

10) Hey, high tech guy, you don't need to shop on Christmas Eve! On Christmas Day create and print a colorful coupon book on your computer. During the year, she can redeem coupons for things you would have shopped for if the bowling league hadn't gobbled up your time. However, if she redeems a coupon within a week of her birthday, mark it in your win column as a twofer.

11) Let her use her greater empathy and sensitivity to do all the shopping for you, family and friends. That will give you time to focus on that special gift—assuming you can find it at the clubhouse.

12) If you think she might forget to give you something you really want like tools, sports equipment, computers or stereo gear, buy it yourself and pretend Santa sent it to you.

Wrong Sports

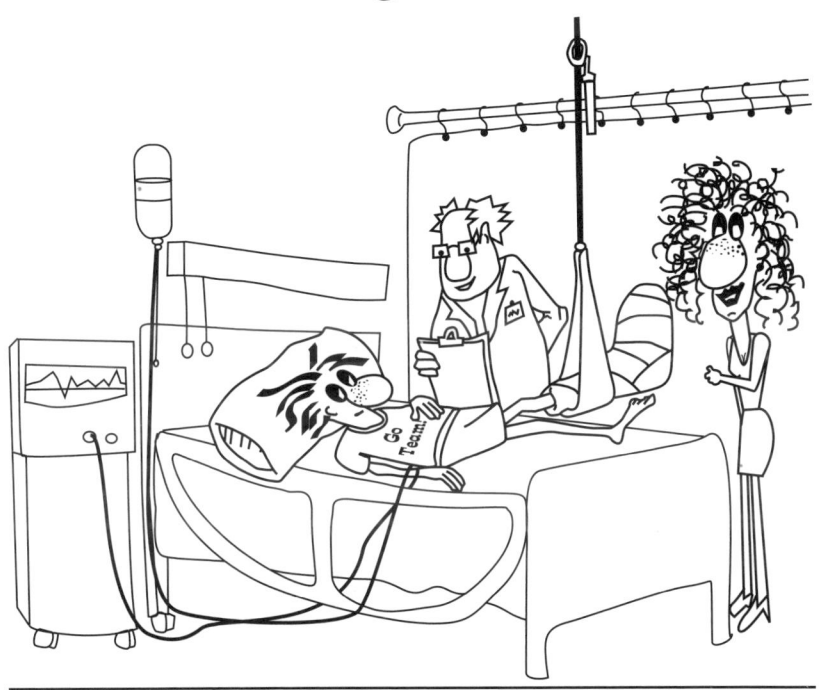

I told him not to "go long" without opening the sliding
glass door first.

I was in the Wrong Sports Emporium the other day. That's
where I go when I want to find new ways to hurt myself in
a socially acceptable fashion. That way I can treat myself to
beer and conversation with other sufferers of sports aches and
pains. For some reason, if it's a sport, we accept that the goal
is to have fun and pain at the same time. Ideally for amateurs,
we accumulate enough aches and pains so work looks like a
vacation spa after the weekend sports bludgeoning.

Currently, the nation is suffering from a treacherous bout
of health consciousness. Some guys take off after work, as well

as on weekends, for the gym, field, water, cliff or trail. They persist in hurting themselves sufficiently to sleep through their jobs—sitting. buddalike until it's time for another bout of wrong sports. You can try to talk sense

> The most dangerous strategy is to jump a chasm in two leaps.
> —Benjamin Disraeli

into the ones who aren't hearing impaired. Remember, the iPod buds glued in guys ears are playing the same music at the same volume level used to torture prisoners of war.

You probably think I am exaggerating. How could this nation be so productive, if the workforce is asleep? It's a good question and you may not like my answers. For one thing, since machines do most of the work now, it is often best if humans stay out of the way. For another, as sports nuts sleep on the job, they are in touch with higher dream states, where the next great invention—wireless high-wire walking—is all the rage. Then, they wake up briefly, type an email or two and voila, a new industry is born.

Even the most avid sportaholic, occasionally suffers moments where we ask ourselves, why we are involved in games where the equipment warns of injury or death—but only if you use it. As we age, guys buy this equipment and store it, in case we wake up younger than yesterday.

Moreover, why would guys create games where not only skill but also real danger is involved—say sky diving, ski jumping and riding a sled down the stairs into a few pillows on the landing. My sons invented this sport while we were out of the house. You take a Flexible Flyer sled upstairs, put your bed pillows at the bottom, get on the sled together and slide down picking up speed in the general direction of the minor emergency ward at the hospital.

They also figured out how to climb along a hallway near the ceiling by pushing against the sidewalls—something like Spiderman. Small handprints gave that game away. Later, they came up with the sport of jumping off the garage roof across six feet of concrete into a swimming pool. One slip and….

Needless to say these children's parental units didn't know about such sports at the time they were invented. Otherwise, the less stable male unit might have joined in the fun. We did suspect something odd when one of the boys broke a bone getting dressed. We suspected they were idiot males no matter how well they tested on intelligence tests. Fortunately, they survived and prospered. Not so fortunate is the gene pool, which will continue to contain guys born to do stupid stuff to get the adrenal glands pumping.

> We did suspect something odd when one of the boys broke a bone getting dressed.

Science Says

This brings us to science, which can point out that one reason men can endure pain for thrills of adventure is they are less sophisticated emotionally. Negative emotions in young children start out in a primitive area of the brain shaped the same in rats and men—the amygdale, according to Leonard Sax in his book *Why Gender Matters*.

In girls, negative emotions are later handled in the more advanced cerebral cortex where language and reasoning is situated. If you can put emotional concerns about dangerous ideas into words and weigh the consequences of your actions, you might be less inclined to leap off cliffs, skateboard into traffic or jump numerous school buses and spend six months in intensive care.

I'm not saying that's why Evel Knievel is a guy and Martha Stewart is a woman, just that matching bedding with wallpaper is somewhat less dangerous than matching ramp speed to flight distance on a motorcycle.

And Martha can say why she does what she does and make some sense out of it. According to Wikipedia (the encyclopedia with the motto, "If it's true, it's not our fault."), Evel Knievel was fired from a surface mining job when he made an earthmover pop a wheelie and drove it into Butte's main power line, leaving the city without electricity for several hours and putting Evel briefly in the slammer. This is primitive amygdale power in action—the same sort of power that results in trauma patients being 75% male (Illinois Trauma Registry).

> ...matching bedding with wallpaper is somewhat less dangerous than matching ramp speed to flight distance...

Martha might also land herself in jail, but she did it over the phone—using that darned cerebral cortex of hers. No one ever accused Evel of using that part of his brain.

Reality TV, which has little or nothing to do with reality but a lot to do with stupidity, has expanded the list of stupid and dangerous things guys can do while cameras are running. We haven't quite descended to the level of the Roman Coliseum, but we are clearly heading that way. It's a form of retro-evolution where we evolve into more and more primitive life forms—eventually turning humanity into teams of protozoa happy to duke it out on a beach, with the winner taking possession of a Trump-Tower-sized load of ooze.

Guys really don't ever get over childhood and sports. They play football, baseball, kick the can, cops and robbers, swordplay with sticks that could poke an eye out, throwing rocks at each other, playing next to raging rivers their mothers thought they never went near and too many other sports to list.

They play sports day and night, night and day, always in competition with other guys. The result in my family (where five boys drove one girl to the convent) was that my mother gave up having anything nice on display. Balls of all kinds flew around the living room at the least provocation, even though the phrase "go long" could mean traveling through plate glass or wallboard—whatever material blocked the shortest route to long.

As I recall, no one died playing ball in the living room, but the cut glass vase sometimes got in the way of an errant pass and gradually took on the chipped-crystal look.

They didn't make enough glue to hold together the ceramics we broke, so at last my mother resorted to the bare-shelf look, letting us test the strength of the furniture and floorboards with our heads. After she purchased the titanium dining décor with bulletproof-glass display cabinet and the Plexiglas shields for TV and windows, she never had another problem—except with the drapes, which we used to swing through the air like Tarzan.

> They didn't make enough glue to hold together the ceramics we broke...

During the winter we played with and broke our trains, toy cars and ping-pong tables. Girls could sometimes join in these games, but they didn't get the same pleasure out of testing the limits of steel and cement with their heads (I'd say "using their heads", but guys try not to do that).

I know a grown man with a dream job. He breaks things for a living to find out how strong they are. If he didn't have to write a lot of data down in reports for his customers, he would never need to take a vacation.

The thing about guys' games is that they nearly always involve competition. Put three boys together with nothing to do and one of them will try jumping off the top of something, and then the others will have to try it, and then one will ask what if they stood on stilts, and…. The game ends when one of them breaks an important body part, dies or distinguishes himself as the bravest of the brave (in female terms the most idiotic of the idiots).

The reason guys do this is testosterwrong makes them want to win at something and anything will do. Thus, guys never stop wanting to play. This has its advantages with kids, because grown men's energy can sometimes be funneled into coaching youth with all the enthusiasm of a child.

...men often don't get it!

The ultimate glory of this is seen in that Kurt Russell movie, "Miracle," about the USA's 1980 Olympic hockey team. The coach works the players nigh onto death but the guys hang in and become a family. Of course, strains appear with the coach's wife as the coach dedicates every moment to his team. But his dedication does buy victory and cheers up the whole country. Then, like every guy, the coach has to face off at home and practice holding, hooking and high sticking with the wife. Fortunately, by then, the movie is over.

When relating to a spouse, we admit it, guys don't get it! They aren't even aware that for their spouse sports do not have a place in kitchen, living room or loft—and especially not between the loft and the formal dining room. Look out! Here comes something now!

Yes, guys actually seem to believe they are right on the subject of sports. In a perfect world, women will come to agree with men that football, wrestling and your smaller motorbike races are for the family room; sex is a lot like tossing a long ball into the end zone, only the huddle is replaced with the 30-second cuddle followed by the 15-second big play; food for all sporting events involves hamburgers and hot dogs or for variation hot dogs and hamburgers; sports clothes are appropriate all year around at all events although at church it's ok to wear shorts instead of a Speedo; and sports analogies apply to everything, everywhere, all the time.

With our combined experience and extensive consultations with guys sitting in bars and bleachers there is evidence that men will continue to inhabit the realm of wrong sports. Meanwhile, we'd appreciate it if women would work on the cheering to chuckling ratio so that there is more cheering at men's remarkable abilities in wrong sports and less chuckling at a few wrong moves now and then—like the time Uncle Harry did the head plant on the sofa, bounced onto his feet on the end table and clunked his head on the ceiling. That might have looked funny, but don't forget—he caught the pass and his team won the big game and the first bite of the cantaloupe they were using for a ball.

...his team won the big game and the first bite of the cantaloupe they were using for a ball.

Shoe Flipping

Wrong Jim enjoys the simple to practice sport of shoe flipping. Once, he was practicing this sport in a living room with friends.

"I said whoops!" Jim reminded them...

Jim's wife, Pat, was situated on the floor next to his legs as he sat above on a couch. Ordinary males might enjoy conversing in the relaxed warmth of such a room, watching the resident male pyromaniac tend the fire. Not so sports-fanatic Jim.

He freed his right foot's size twelve orthopedic oxford, lifted it and gave it a tentative flip. He advanced his technique until at last he could flip his shoe an incredible three revolutions—without leaving heel marks on the ceiling. He kept at it until he missed the catch. Gravity pounded the shoe into Pat's head. Jim was now firmly planted in the Land of Wrong. But he was able to move it up a notch by his nonplussed response. "Whoops!" he said.

His friends immediately attacked him. "At least apologize!" they urged.

"I said whoops!" Jim reminded them.

That shut them up. Who can argue with whoops! Whoops is a guy admitting he was wrong—something rare and good and beautiful. Such a moment would only be marred by a maudlin, "I'm sorry." Jim's friends were so wrong!

Martial Arts

Please forgive me. When it comes to fighting, I prefer techniques that involve ducking and dodging to those that require actual physical contact with a sweaty, bacteria-ridden opponent.

Where a true tough guy might proudly wear a t-shirt emblazoned with the word "Dangerous" (careful tough guys, Michael's song is about a tough girl) I prefer my t-shirt to read "Attack me slowly, I know tai chi."

I was attracted to the slow and graceful movements of tai chi. However, I was snookered. Every move in tai chi is designed to do onto others as you would not have them do onto you.

Still, tai chi fits my style. The idea is to deflect the force of a thousand pounds with a few ounces of effort—a goal I can sign up to.

> The idea is to deflect the force of a thousand pounds with a few ounces of effort—a goal I can sign up to.

I particularly like a move called snake creeps down, as opposed to the move called snake creeps me out— which is not a martial arts move at all but more of an issue when swimming with water moccasins.

Where in American boxing does the boxer slide one foot forward until he looks like he is about to do the splits, except his other leg is bent in half so his butt is almost on the floor and that bent knee is about to knock his false teeth out?

If you can do this move and rise without requiring a hip replacement, most opponents will run—for a straight jacket. If you don't get up, hope they run for a doctor. Sometimes, six months of traction is all that is needed to repair the damage, which reminds me. I not only know snake creeps down, I know how to…

Do Traction at Home

Millions of American's, both sports enthusiasts and couch potato enthusiasts suffer back problems. Fortunately, my father provided me the example of do-it-yourself traction. (I'd tell you not to try this at home, but where else would you try it?)

Once, Dad strained his back to such an extent that he couldn't straighten up, and one leg appeared shorter than the other. He tried aspirin, doctors and Swedish massage. Everything helped a bit, but still he looked like the walking wounded.

One doctor recommended traction. Dad had a mechanical bent—he pressed and probed to find out how they would do it. That night, Dad located what he would need—one partially filled can of paint, a dish towel to tie around his ankle and an extension cord to use as a rope between the paint can and the well secured dish towel. (If you don't have an extra extension cord, you could always cut the cord that opens and closes the blinds and use that).

> In the morning, he gave himself a brain transplant and has been fine ever since.

Dad climbed into bed in his hunched over painful condition. Since he might well have killed us if we laughed out loud at his self-administered cure, we retreated from the scene and only heard about it later.

The weight pulled on his leg, but he needed the other foot pressed against the footboard to keep from falling out of bed. So, he rigged up a rope from the headboard to a belt he attached above his back pain—around his neck for all I know.

Thus equipped, he put traction on his leg. In the morning, he gave himself a head transplant and has been fine ever since. Actually, he was a little better in the morning and the morning after that. So, the home remedy worked. All I can add is: Don't try this at the office unless you have a very large desk.

This high risk approach to healing—undoubtedly gave me the courage to try…

Acupuncture for Cheapskates

True, acupuncture is an art and science developed over thousands of years and based on a theory of energy flow through meridians that relate to the body's main organs—but not in any obvious way. Maybe your gall bladder meridian is low on energy so you stick a needle in your head or arm or leg, not your gall bladder. Go figure.

…find something that works for the pain, so you can continue hurting yourself…

You could spend years learning the complexities of this system. But there is a short cut that in Wrong Jim's opinion works just fine for treating sports aches and pains. You find a sore place on your body and put a needle there. One caution: remove the needles before resuming the sport or dressing for dinner.

You wouldn't do this if you weren't a guy. What if you happened to needle the spot I saw dramatized in a movie, where a needle stuck in a guy's body magically kills him? Of course, if such a place existed, the actor would have been dead. But couldn't a bumbling idiot male do himself harm by healing his sports-produced aches and pains without seeking FDA approval of the wrong approach he is trying. Of course he could. Thus, life provides an endless supply of wrong males in hopes some of them survive and advise their children to seek professional help for what ails them.

Hopefully some of the help for wrong guys will be psychological. Guys need to change the attitude that they can do wrong sports before removing the cast they are wearing from doing wrong sports.

We realize that guys will continue to love sports, including wrong sports. So, our advice is simple: Find something for the pain. Then, keep playing sports you are too old to play, before you are too old to play them.

Oh, and forget that grow old gracefully stuff. That's for people who insist on walking around gingerly on two sore feet. No, don't try to preserve your body when you can abuse it and then buy one of those motorized wheelchairs when your body decides the time has come to refuse to move instead of refusing to lose.

> Guys need to change the attitude that they can do wrong sports before removing the cast they are wearing from doing wrong sports.

The medical profession keeps promising to keep us wrong guys going. There are reports that soon doctors will be able to repair cartilage. This is an urgent need, since normal wear and tear can result in joints with bone banging on bone.

You could caution the young to take care of their bodies, but we know that won't happen, as long there is a chance of winning a trophy and playing a game you enjoy. So medicine is trying to figure out how to build joint scaffolding where new cartilage can grow. Won't that be great? Then, guys at ninety-nine can still jog, as long as they can remember where they put their hearing aides, glasses, jogging shoes and that pallet load of aspirin.

Sinus Buster

Wrong Jim was always plagued with allergies and related sinus problems. At times these hindered his ability to participate in wrong sports, but only if they involved going outdoors. Of course, he tried all the over the counter and prescription drugs. He even yearned for under the counter drugs, if they would rid him of nagging allergies. No luck.

Naturally, Jim was excited to hear recently about an alternative medicine for allergies and related headaches. What's more, the alternative was clearly invented by a wrong guy, since he had named it Sinus Buster, not Sinus Aid, or Sinus Relief or Sinus Salvation. The idea of busting sinus problems in the nose with powerful macho weaponry appealed to Jim. What's more, the inventor discovered his cure by accident—do wrong guys do things any other way?

Former self-defense teacher, Wayne Perry, volunteered to be hit by pepper spray for a video to show his classes. The day of the shoot a cluster headache was on the way. One shot of pepper spray in the face and the headache disappeared.

I heard about this from Jan Stack-Leuze, a woman who is helping with the layout of this book and who has a scar from sinus surgery that says she should know sinus trouble when she sniffs it. She likes the stuff.

Being Wrong Jim, I figured I didn't need Wayne Perry when there was plenty of pepper in the world. So I mixed my own brew and in no time I had clogged up a metered spray bottle I was using. Also, in spite of getting some pepper up my nose, I developed a sinus infection and needed antibiotics to survive long enough to write this.

Nevertheless, I plan to try the real Sinus Buster, because I'm a wrong guy and the name is remarkably wrong. Jan points out to me that you can feel it work. It could be a hot product for some time to come. In some future wrong book, I'll reveal whether I have to come up with a new excuse not to exercise, because my sinus problems are forever cured. It could happen.

> He recommended that I buy his mother a self-defense spray and have her use it on me—a very wrong idea...

Now, I should add that in my family is a brilliant physician and sinus specialist (possibly a biased opinion). He mentioned a host of ideas for resolving allergies and none of them included Sinus Buster. Then, son number two weighed in. He is an equally brilliant engineer and quickly figured out a two-for-one strategy. He recommended that I buy his mother a self-defense spray and have her use it on me—a very wrong idea that I was immediately drawn to like a moth to candle flame.

Pat's response surprised me. "If I had pepper spray, you would have borrowed it and tried it out."

What can I say? A man who saw part of this book said it best, "You knew you married Mrs. Right. You didn't know her first name was Always." The truth hurts. So, does the pepper spray!

Extreme Sports

We've nodded in the direction of extreme sports in our anecdotes of family and friends, but now it is time to focus in a manly way on extreme sports. How much more wrong can you get than to take part in a Warren Miller ski movie, or an X games championship for skateboarding, wakeboarding or driving a snowmobile very fast across a river not quite covered with ice (something guys in the Mid-West are said to actually do for fun).

Let's take only one example and try to understand what is going on in the heads of the men and (definitely fewer) women who participate in these sports. Take, for example, extreme kayaking. The person who has the current record in the sport is still living—Tao Berman of Oregon. In 1999, he dropped 98 feet 4 inches down a waterfall in Canada. I'll bet those last four inches were really hard.

Since then, Tao has done other dumb or marvelous things in his kayak like a speed altitude descent 300 feet down a chute into two or three feet of water. Tao says on his web site www.taoberman.com, "When I am extreme kayaking I don't feel fear. That allows me to be the best that I can be, because emotion doesn't get in the way of what I want to run."

The only thing we can add is that emotion also doesn't get in the way of dead people's decisions. Whether or not you want to do things that prove you are as unemotional as wallboard all depends on whether testosterone warped your brain in the womb. While we assume Tao will live as long as Evel Knieval, like Evel, Tao occasionally faces the downer of recovering from injuries, which prevents him playing with danger all the time.

Guys like Tao are a breed apart. Ordinary men and women would get injured and realize they could learn accounting. Tao feels about his risky activities much the way we feel about drinking an extra latte at Starbucks once in awhile—confident, fearless and slightly warm.

Now, I said I would write about one example of extreme sports and I did. But it occurs to me that Spike TV has offered a show that deserves mention. I mean *MXC*, which somehow stands for *Most Extreme Elimination Challenge*. They used *MXC* as the initials because the actual acronym (MEEC) could be read as MEEK, which would give the wrong impression—definitely wrong, definitely.

> Real people ...ride down waterslides in large but unstable teacups... and fall into muddy, yucky and possibly disease-ridden water.

This show was created in Japan and although a few Yankees have insinuated their formerly healthy bodies into the mayhem, it is still pretty much a Japanese show mistranslated into American with a wrong and slightly off-color attitude—actually, the show's translation pushes toward a raunchy rating, but the talk is really not the point. Real people of mixed athletic skill run gauntlets, ride down waterslides in large but unstable teacups, or fling themselves through the air at a Velcro wall and stick to it or miss and fall into muddy, yucky and possibly disease-ridden water.

Where Tao Berman is a thrill seeker, these teams of people do this for fun or team building or because they recently acquired large life insurance policies that will make their descendants rich as soon as they kill themselves without legally committing suicide.

We propose giving the creators of this show and everyone associated with it a black belt in wrong. Since women participate in the stupidity, we will have to invent the first female black belt in wrong—which will still be black but might have a pink belt buckle or something and be created by a designer instead of a bored hardware store employee.

Firewalking, Flow and the Zone

Twice, I did firewalking. That's where you remove your head so you can think with your feet. The leader guided us through some games and experiences to show the power of intention. Then we did it. Some have argued that the reason this is possible is because wood ash is a good insulator. Let me say in favor of that argument that the ash feels much like crunching over snow, but warmer. I can't help thinking something like adrenaline is involved—the chemical that allows petite women to lift cars off their pet Chihuahua.

The physics involved are simple: $E = MC2$ where E stands for energy, M stands for masochists and C stands for hot coals. You might want to divide by I for idiots and multiply by LD for love danger. I'm not sure how it works, but I'm sure that it occasionally sends people to the emergency ward.

The reason you do wrong stuff like going over waterfalls in kayaks and walking on hot coals is because you can then tell yourself and others that you accomplished one of the really stupid things in the world and are still alive. This assumes that you are still alive.

In a previous life I did impossible stuff. That only left silly stuff to explore...

Also, you can begin to feel that if you can do something dangerous you can do anything. I'm still trying to apply this theory to walking through walls. I've had success, especially where there are doorways. I've also written a book about wrong. Maybe, I have been here before. In a previous life, I did impossible stuff. That only left silly stuff to explore and voila—*The Theory of Wrong* was born.

Mihaly Csikszentmihalyi has written *Flow: The Psychology of Optimal Experience*. Being in flow is like Michael Jordan being in the zone, like Tao Berman successfully negotiating a dangerous waterfall or like anyone caught up in a totally engrossing activity—let's say pumpkin carving or picking blackberries without the thorns scratching you to death.

They become liquid and flow by defenses like a river flows by rocks.

When in flow, we have a sense of confidence and we get immediate feedback on how we are doing—thorn pricks in our example. Our focus is so intense there is no room for emotion or outside thoughts to interfere with our performance. The passage of time is distorted. You hear of athletes talking about the game slowing down. You see basketball players making move after move while in the air on the way to a basket. How do they do it? They become liquid and flow by defenses like a river flows by rocks.

Prisoners of war have found ways to get into flow by going on imaginary journeys or considering every aspect of their cell in great detail, where the materials came from and how they were put together. One man emerged from prison to immediately play an excellent game of golf. He had mentally played golf every day in prison.

For me, snow skiing has the elements of flow. Like water you follow the fall line, developing skill to handle bumps and falling bodies scattered around the hill like pepper on fried egg white. You discover you can go an entire day without worrying about work or relationships—especially if your wife skis at her pace and you ski at yours. That only leaves lunchtime to get in trouble by saying the wrong thing.

Experiences of flow are available in activities like games, sewing and carpentry, where a mistake provides the same sort of instant feedback as a painful fall does at the edge of physical skill. Flow is available to everyone—rich and poor, healthy and physically challenged.

Oddly, the number one leisure activity nowadays is watching TV, which is seldom if ever capable of getting us into flow. So although we have suggested that guys are wrong to do dangerous or extreme sports, we now come face to face with facts: wrong sports can be a reason for living—when they don't kill you.

> Sports can be a reason for living— when they don't kill you.

Professional Sports

It would be wrong to leave a chapter on sports without mentioning professional sports. There, I feel better. We are talking about all the thrill of victory and agony of defeat stuff available on TV, in stadiums and at the office for players of fantasy football.

The thing women sense from the outset and guys seldom get is the proportion of agony to thrills in professional sports is heavily weighted toward agony.

For example, each year 32-football teams strive to win the Super Bowl. One team wins. Consequently, the fan spends year after year living in agony, while men in one region are thrilled for one year, occasionally more. In fact, only a little over half of the teams have ever won a single Superbowl. That means most of the country is in agony year after year.

Then add sports fans' agony to the agony of amateur golfers who hit one shot worthy of Tiger Woods for every 100 shots we hit like the hackers we are.

Now add that to the general agony of the body that results from playing sports and you have a nation in agony all of the time.

Thus, the blues are an endlessly popular form of music invented by slaves but suited to sportaholics. Another form of music suited to agony is rap. The very word sounds like something the first grade teacher did to your knuckles with a ruler. The music knows sports, life and wrong. Listen to the music.

In fact, several people are drug and alcohol free and high on life...

You might expect that the entire nation must be drinking beer and taking medication to fight off the agony of defeat. In fact, several people are drug and alcohol free and high on life.

Apparently, these folks move around every year so they can support the team that just won the Super Bowl.

Wrong Bridge

Men sometimes let a sport or game become a monomania. Our male brains love to focus and dig through layers of rules, angles, techniques, laws and situations until zeal leads to skill and finally to mastery. Then mastery needs to be exercised and honed until a guy is best in the world or at least in one hemisphere— usually the right (or spatial) hemisphere of a male brain.

Hal's brain had mastered bridge to such an extent that his trophies were crowding the living room and his wife Joan viewed the time away from family and work as excessive. Still, Hal couldn't stop himself from collecting more and more master points.

Finally, Joan rebelled and forbid Hal from playing bridge. Admittedly, he owed her this after once forgetting her on a Canadian road trip for seven hours. However, Hal found it difficult to let go of the thrill of victory.

One day, Joan was driving Hal's car. She moved the seat forward and it stuck. She couldn't drive that way and she persisted. At last, the seat jumped forward and launched a golden bridge trophy in the general direction of the brake pedal—she checked the victory date and immediately realized it would take more counseling to break Hal of his bridge habit.

Wrong Socks (or Tennis)

Sports aren't always for fun (I guess we have previously suggested they are never for fun, but we are probably wrong). When playing golf or tennis with the boss or a client, another layer of complexity is added. Lose and your boss might wonder why he hired an incompetent; win and your client's ego might shrivel up and blow away.

One day, Wrong Bob was successfully negotiating these hazards, making sure his athletic boss, Guy, ate a few Bo Jangles Country Home Biscuits before an early morning round of tennis. That evened things out. However, this day after a quick shower, Bob realized he forgot dress socks. Rather than commit a fashion faux pas, he slipped naked feet into wingtips and figured he could fake it.

You lose and your boss might wonder why he hired an incompetent.

The morning went fine—a series of meetings with an important client failed to reveal any naked ankles. But when client, George, decided he needed to add a quart of oil to his well traveled car, Bob saw a chance. He navigated to a Big K and while George headed off for oil, Wrong Bob sought socks.

Things would have been fine, except Bob had no way to pay for the socks, because his mind was in another galaxy that day, along with his wallet. George paid for the socks, but became curious and Bob confessed.

Back at work, George set up a company-wide Bob Heck's Sock Fund by sticking an envelope onto a prominently displayed notice board, where many employees could contribute to sock-deprived Bob.

The next day, Bob walked into work late after some off-site meetings and everyone was happy to see him, judged by the giggles he elicited everywhere he went.

Wrong Jim discovered a similarly embarrassing sport. He was in his office when he got a call from his boss. He walked across a parking lot to her building and found several co-workers waiting with her. It finally dawned on him that the sport was watching a guy perform wrong dressing.

Jim was wearing his sweater inside out. Had he not been sleepwalking, he might have pointed out to his tormentors that this was a new fashion trend.

Instead, he tried the old I'm-too-busy-to-be-bothered-with-such-nonsense. When that didn't work, he turned the sweater right side out to major applause and made a grand exit with cheeks flushed as red as the sweater he was wearing.

Jim spent the rest of his life waiting for Bob to invent the Theory of Wrong, which would point out that they were both wrong because they were guys—so not to worry.

...everyone was happy to see him, it seemed, judged by the smiles and giggles his mere appearance elicited...

Notes from the
Cup o' Wrong Café

Sports Rules

1) If it doesn't hurt, maybe you're not doing it right.

2) If the warning label threatens death, it's probably fun until you lose consciousness.

3) The way to tell if you are in shape for a sports activity is if you are breathing.

4) Going high in the air is fun, coming down is fun, landing can be hard—but two parts fun to one part pain is life all over.

5) On the other hand, no pain, no pain.

6) To the victor go the spoils—so come in second. That way you won't win anything rotten.

7) Go long, but open the sliding-glass door first.

8) Winning isn't the only thing, there's dumping ice-cold Gatorade on the coach outdoors in January.

9) If your team wins, have a beer to celebrate.

10) If your team loses, have a beer to commiserate.

11) Short on pain medication? Stick some needles where it hurts. You'll feel much better when you take them out.

12) Ask your senators to outlaw the agony of defeat.

13) Sports Paradox: Keep playing sports you are too old to play, before you are too old to play them.

Mr. Fix It Wrong

Wrong Hardware

Home Destruction Kit

"He said it has everything we need."

Men's ability to fix things wrong is legendary. Of course, men read directions as a last resort. In our wrong view, reading directions is like holding a crib sheet in your lap during the big exam—it's cheating. Directions remind us of nagging parents telling us to tie our shoes and not to forget our lunch. Who needs that—until lunchtime?

Besides, you'll never find fresh solutions, if you slavishly follow what some other guy tells you in three languages on a flimsy sheet of folded paper—even if that guy designed the gizmo you are currently breaking. With a little creative genius, you might turn that modular furniture kit into a modern sculpture. Who says shelves have to lead dull lives holding stuff? Line them up as partial paneling for walls or on the floor as a pathway that simultaneously saves on carpet wear and tests your tripping quotient.

Also, hiding the stuff you broke in the attic or garage is good exercise. So, we recommend that you immediately toss any instructions, lest you be tempted to confer with them. Of course, keep in mind, you are reading a book by wrong guys.

Always remember, everything you need to solve every problem around the house—except how to get along with your spouse—is at the Wrong Hardware Store. They have duct tape, masking tape, strapping tape, metal tape and Teflon tape. For those who like to do things by the book, they have measuring tape. They have epoxy, silicone and carpenter's glue. They have rivets, screws, nails and various tools for hurting yourself in ways you hadn't thought of before—torches, nail guns (did you see the x-rays of that guy who accidentally shot a nail up his nose?), drills (good for brain surgery), and wrenches (a wrenching time for a guy isn't emotionally draining but more of a physical strength test).

> The first rule to tinkering is to save all the parts.
> —Paul Erlich

Most guys have some talent at fixing stuff and solving problems as independent agents—sometimes referred to as household terrorists. If they can fix something without literally bringing down the house, it should rate a passing grade on the report card the wife keeps in her head.

It's not that all men are all stupid all the time—no it's that they are really smart at work and forget that their expertise doesn't apply outside their specialty—take for example, the farmer repairing the combine with bailing wire, the explosives expert fishing with dynamite or the electrical engineer fixing a furnace—this last genius helped create the digital revolution and the furnace fiasco in the same timeframe.

Wrong Jim purchased a house from the electrical engineer. Later, when the furnace didn't work, Jim was about to fix it but was under strict orders not to fix anything else, until he could afford insurance on at least the Pacific Northwest region. Consequently, he contacted a professional who explained that one of the electric heating elements had been running 24-hours a day—winter and summer—thanks to that genius engineer's repairs. It was a lesson for Wrong Jim in how smart guys can completely screw things up. Up to that point, he assumed stupid people were responsible. Ah, but stupid people could have humility and therefore wisdom. Smart people are the ones to watch out for. They think they know even when they don't. Based on this wrong IQ test, we must be smart guys, since we are so often wrong.

Before Wrong Jim moved into the house with the funny furnace, he sold the house with the drippy faucet. Of course, he knew how to fix a faucet. He bought another one and installed it. The rest of the story is insurance claim history.

When the new owners didn't move into the house immediately, the basement filled with water from the leak

> It was a lesson for Wrong Jim in how smart guys can completely screw things up.

on the second story—providing the lucky family with a big enough insurance claim to remodel the house and replace the shag carpet and dated wood paneling.

But, let's be honest. Men don't always fix things wrong. In fact, men created virtually all of the so-called wonders of the world: the wall, the floor and the gravity-defying ceiling—not to mention pyramids, cathedrals and the paper clip. Meanwhile, women created clothing, the diet to fit into the clothing and the broom to sweep cobwebs off the ceiling.

Actually, a woman's idea of a wonder of the world would be an extended family where everyone got along. It could happen, but she isn't holding her breath.

For women, it's all about relationships, for men, it's about stuff—organizing it, mixing it with other stuff and standing well back in case something unexpected happens—like the Nerf football derails the model train, which falls into the home brew, which spills on one of the extension cords from the workbench—creating a short, which turns off the power, which leaves our hero in the dark, where he stumbles over a glass jar and strikes a match to see if it was the jug of apple cider or the one with the power to launch the basement into the ionosphere, where he opens a branch office to further explore the Theory of Wrong.

But much as men are known for brilliant inventions—like the blog, reality TV and the rubber chicken—they also occasionally come up with really dumb stuff—like the blog, reality TV and the barbecued rubber chicken—not to mention the whoopee cushion hidden in the seat of honor.

Guys are always fixing everything except their relationships with their spouses, which are pretty much beyond repair at the moment. This is because men's brains are designed to ignore distractions like children, pets and the unbalanced checkbook—so they can focus on new uses for duct tape, bungee cords and the lumps of gum under the chair—I hope that's gum down there.

A woman's idea of a wonder of the world would be an extended family where everyone got along.

As a result, men—even ordinary men like us—have accomplished some amazing things—for example, using tape and screws to fix flip-flops, a butter knife to replace a dead bolt at the house where Wrong Jim grew up and a squirt of WD-40 to repair the squeak in the steering wheel of the car. One squirt of lubricant and voila—no more squeaks! Also, no more cruise control or horn due to short circuits in those systems.

Yes, friends, the same problem-solving genius that builds rocket ships and surgical tools is often available for work around the home. So, my wrong advice is to free the untutored-tinkering genius of the household from the deadweight of conventional thinking.

Those in the know realize how stupid it would be to do what the ignorant do without hesitation...

Remember, it was just such a tinkerer who came up with the xerographic process in his kitchen—with a little help later from some engineer guys who knew stuff. But too much knowledge is a sobering thing. It kills innovation. If it didn't, the guys who know stuff wouldn't need the discoveries of ignorant inventive geniuses. Those in the know realize how stupid it would be to do what the ignorant do without hesitation—and often without accident insurance.

You have only to glance at the film of early attempts at flight to realize how many ignorant geniuses launched themselves off hills, ladders and barns in whimsical attempts to fly. The whimsy faded some for those who killed themselves, but the attempts continued.

You begin to appreciate that the Wright brothers were pretty special bicycle repairmen. The whimsy lives on in many average guys as they attempt home repairs. The phrases "don't do this at home" and "don't do it yourself" cannot be repeated enough by women who care about a) their mates or b) self-preservation.

Yet, consider that your man could be a Wright brother with an idea about to take flight. And guys being guys, there is a good chance that if a wife sends her husband to fix the clothes dryer, he might invent a new kind of cotton candy machine or an exercise wheel for the family pet.

I think the glory of my own genetic legacy was expressed in my Father's work at a lake cabin. Back when he and my Uncle propped up the lake place, building a cabin was equivalent to being a gunman in the Wild West. There was a sense of freedom, unbounded by foolish laws or conventional building codes. One can still see this approach flourish in country plots, farms and superfund waste cleanup sites.

...your man could be a Wright brother with an idea about to take flight.

Rube Goldberg gave his name to the whimsy of male genius that can make the simple job done right into the complicated job done with whatever is handy. So it was at the family lake cabin.

The first dock was made of found logs bound with cables and decked with found boards. The whole job took a weekend and floated but you wouldn't want to wear shoes and socks on it. It was a low-rider for sure, inviting ripples to wash across it like they were ocean waves. Later, a boat moorage area was added—where parts from Dad's boat-trailer business were welded together helter-skelter to support a roof slightly more level than a sloped hillside.

When a certain Idaho county decided to bring the septic systems at the lake up to code, Dad hired the job done. Low and behold, a car was unearthed from the backyard. The contractor's horror increased when he asked what the car was doing there. Dad confessed, in male fashion, that it was serving as the septic tank, but it wasn't his fault—his brother-in-law did it.

Actually, the buried car was an improvement over previous attempts to deal with septic problems—just as the septic system is an uphill walk to the eventual sewage treatment plant.

When Dad tired of beautifying the outdoors (and the flowers he planted were lovely), he took steady aim at the kitchen. In his later years, when perhaps he or my mother should have known better, he designed an attractive kitchen counter area that looked more like House and Garden than lean-to

When Dad tired of beautifying the outdoors, he took steady aim at the kitchen.

lake cabin. Fortunately, for our purposes here, he added some whimsy to the design. He set a special oversized toggle switch on that board that always goes in front of the sink. It operated the disposal and was certainly convenient. Unfortunately, we soon discovered its downside—it could pop on without warning as you leaned over the sink. What an eye-opener it can be at sunrise to have the disposal roar to life unexpectedly like the hungry flesh-eating monster it is.

Another of Dad's innovations included a back-splash behind the sink made of narrow sliding glass. Here, behind water spots, we kept a few small glasses handy. Above the water spots was a bar area with barstools. Under the barstools were glass display-case doors and shelves where some sort of kick plate or foot rail might otherwise go. It was bold design on the loose— a display case at the ready, should humans ever develop eyes in front of their knees.

With this genetic legacy, was it any wonder that I felt free to invent my own rocking chair? True, after a short sit, the person gradually slid to the floor, but the chair was nice to look at and American in its insistent theme that we be always up and doing.

> ...the parts were having most of the fun watching the amateur repairman fuss and fume...

Doing-it-yourself saves money. It also requires endless patience and scheduling skills. Once, Wrong Bob decided to fix the brakes on the car on the day of an important dinner out. Even with an early morning start, getting all the old parts off the car and the new parts in the car didn't quite go as scheduled. In the first place, guessing at the car's model number led to buying slightly wrong parts. This was discovered after the tires, rims and wheels were off and sitting around the driveway having their own rusty spittoon party.

In fact, the parts were having most of the fun watching the amateur repairman fuss and fume, while they seemed to him to be making snide remarks behind his back. It might be embarrassing for an auto repairman to ask for a ride to dinner, but sometimes it's the only option.

Home Improvement

The entertainment world finally nodded in the direction of Mr. Fix It Wrong with Tim Allen's show about Tim Taylor, a family guy who stars in his own TV show called Tool Time. During Tool Time, Tim continually fixes things wrong, while his partner Al, played by Richard Karn, calmly saves the day.

Tim Taylor became famous for applying the Binford 480—most powerful tool known to man—to jobs where something closer to a dentist drill might have worked. The show explored a wrong guy charging full bore into the teeth of a problem and becoming his own worst enemy. Still available in reruns, the show can help those looking for ideas on how to destroy stuff in the process of repairing it—and do it in mucho macho fashion.

The other TV show that captures wrong guys doing it themselves in ridiculous style is of course Red Green, starring Steve Smith. The show frequently demonstrates the value of the handyman's helper—duct tape. Red uses it to fix a flat tire by taping a good tire to the flat, for example. Of course, he had no choice. The lug nuts were rusted in place. Red has spent 15 seasons exploring wrong guys and dishing out humorous advice on relationships, while showing how to fix things wrong. We highly recommend this show to those who can't figure out how to be wrong males on their own.

We doubt that these two shows have exhausted the possibilities for humor shows about Mr. Fix It Wrong. For example, we can imagine a documentary show that would wander this incredible country exploring things like a school bus I saw once on the California coast.

While we parked ourselves in a motel and explored the beach, the bus parked for a night on a beachside road. A wood stove warmed things up in the morning—smoke rising out the stack. Part of the bus had been cut away and replaced with a wood hut-like structure sided with shingles.

To a guy, it looked like a beautiful mobile home and a beautiful life, although looks can be deceptive. To most women, it would look moderately junky and fine for someone else, if health codes were observed and no one was forced against their will to live there.

Wrong guys don't need Detroit or anyone else to show them how to cobble together unique vehicles, craft floaty things that expand the definition of boats, or turn a tree into a tree house or several co-located trees into a tree apartment complex with connecting rope swings or rope and board walkways. The building codes for such things need to be carefully ignored so that creativity is given free and wrong reign.

The Water Leak That Proved Bob Wrong

There are men so wise they don't even try to fix it wrong. Bob wasn't so wrong the day he chose to impress Alayne by showing he trusted her completely—especially her networking skills, which produced a handy list of phone numbers for plumbers, painters, carpet layers, electricians and renovation experts that she used for several rental units they owned.

So, one morning, Wrong Bob awoke and prepared for a morning golf game with a business associate. Then, he heard it—a strange hissing noise. He searched but he couldn't see the source.

Stepping outside, he slipped on wet lawn. He opened a basement door to see water rising. He rushed and shut off all water to the house.

Disaster averted, he calmly went inside to tell Alayne that she had a problem. Then, he waved goodbye and drove off to meet his business buddies. Actually, although his empathy remained well hidden, this worked out well, because professionals did the job right.

> ...he calmly went inside to tell Alayne she had a problem...

No doubt testosterwrong and the limited family budget make men think they can always fix things themselves cheaper than people who do this work for a living. Obviously, they sometimes succeed or Home Depot would go out of business. But we recommend that men consider that they are professionals at some job. Whenever possible, do that and let other professionals do their thing.

Now that we've got that straight, where did I put the screws for the electrical panel? Whoops! Darn. I guess I'll write the rest of the book in the dark.

Notes from the
Cup o' Wrong Café

Fix it tips for the king of the castle or the mole of the moat:

- If you hook the cold water up to the hot shower faucet, don't fix it. The shock and surprise will wake up guests and may even save their lives later in the morning when they try to walk down the broken steps as they escape to their car.

- If the electrician hooks up your outdoor light so it is always on, don't fix that either. Think of it as a signal to all that a light among men lives inside.

- Just because everyone else's front door opens into the house doesn't mean yours can't open out. That way you can clunk visitors on the noggin while appearing to be opening the door to welcome them.

- Always epoxy the loose knobs onto the stove so they won't come off when the wife tries to remove them for the grandkids' visit. Instead, jack the stove up on boxes so it is too high for the kiddies to reach.

- Jackhammer a nice hole in the floor under the car, in case you want to change the oil without putting the drain-plug back in.

- Black tape on the dashboard can cover up all those sensor lights that keep going off without saying anything important like 'check engine' or 'low coolant.' Who needs that stuff?

  If she says the relationship has gone stale, she probably just wants a kitchen remodel and a new portable bun warmer.

Foolish Rules and Tools

- If it's worth doing, it's worth doing wrong.

- If she says your relationship is broken, apply glue (hugs) and clamp (hold) for fifteen minutes.

- Maybe the reason she doesn't trust your do-it-yourself repairs is because you keep fixing what isn't broken and breaking what can't be fixed.

- Emergency Room Visit 405: I wonder if you could make a weed whacker out of a ¼" drill, a circular saw blade, some duck tape, and a broomstick?

- If you are dumb enough to sleep under a tree of ripe fruit and an apple hits you in the head, invent the theory of gravity to explain the bump to your wife.

- If the cookie crumbles, get out the glue gun.

- Question: What's the difference between your wife and a nuclear reactor? Answer: You can operate a reactor.

- If you're up a creek without a paddle, get back in the 4 x 4 and drive home.

- Question: Why can't women be more like men? Answer: Because there wouldn't be enough room in the garage for his toys and hers.

- Question: Why can't men be more like women? Answer: Because they'd get lipstick on their booger finger.

- Emergency Room Visit 983: I wonder what would happen if you replaced those worn out snow ski bindings with cup hooks and bungee cords?

- If parts of your relationship don't fit, get a bigger hammer.

Putting the Wrong Foot Forward

You have a bad feeling? But we can't turn back, not when
my X3000 GPS system says we are less than 50 yards
from the view of a lifetime!

If you were even slightly alive in grade school, you no doubt learned about Columbus—the guy who discovered a city in Ohio, where no one had previously thought to look. This required courage to set out on uncharted seas in search of a sea route to Indiana, I think—the place with all the computer help desks and Madras-plaid shirts.

Don't tell Ms. Columbus, but her guy never found Indiana. He would have made it but his gold doubloons wouldn't fit in the expressway tollbooths. Columbus was the first guy to go the right way and end up in the wrong place—or was that Adam?

Nowadays, we know that nothing is as it seems. Columbus wasn't the first to discover America. The mosquitoes were here already—along with the descendents of folks who walked from China and the bones of Leif Erickson. Still, coming here always has required an adventurous spirit—unless you had the good fortune to fly first class.

Without courageous guys willing to do simultaneously crazy and remarkable things, we wouldn't have a clue how to cross an ocean in a wooden boat, cure scurvy and repair a rotator cuff or Achilles tendon. If the doctor is a wrong guy, there is a chance he will repair the Achilles tendon on the patient with the rotator cuff problem. If

A venturesome minority will always be eager to get off on their own... let them take risks...let them get lost, sun burnt, stranded, drowned, eaten by bears... that is the right and privilege of any free American.

—Idaho Law Review 1980.

the patient is a wrong guy, he might not notice. The thing is, guys hurl themselves into adventures to hurt themselves and advance medical science. Either that, or they go on adventures to get out of the house and hurt themselves because no woman is around saying, "Careful, watch your step, look both ways, it might be icy, better duck."

Some guys and gals don't probe the limits of danger but instead trace the limits of human endurance—Lance Armstrong, for example, and people who watch reality TV.

Science supports our idea that guys are willing to venture in any old direction and ignore all the signs of danger ahead because they view every path as their friend.

In general, men and male rats (some women think they are interchangeable) are good at navigating by direction alone, ignoring landmarks that women are better at remembering—like turn left at Starbucks in the mall. Then, Starbucks builds three more stores in the mall and the landmark method no longer works. Meanwhile, the guys have made a killing on the stock. Even if the guys too are lost, they used a different method to end up in the mall's sports bar, when they were supposedly seeking socks.

We see guys exercising their adventuresome spirit all the time. Confidence oozes out of us. We refuse to ask for directions because all we have to do is circumnavigate the globe and we are sure to find the darn place we were looking for—unless we were supposed to go north instead of west to get to the Grizzly Tavern.

> The surprising thing about young fools is how many survive to be old fools.
> —Doug Larson

Oh well, the Brown Bear Tavern will work just as well—plus we didn't know there was a Brown Bear Tavern or that the bartender knows a shortcut to the Grizzly Tavern. So, we kill two birds with one tank of gas—and get a cold beverage to boot. That's how guys are—confident although the floodwaters are rising, the ark has sprung a leak and the wife has a new infinite-limit charge card.

It isn't only geography where men's confidence and perseverance—combined with timely medical attention—lead them to brilliant insights. Remember a guy figured out the fastest way to light a barbecue and ended up with a pile of molten metal in the backyard. A guy grasped how to catapult cows, cars and commodes. It was probably a guy who invented unboat races between collections of junk that float nearly long enough to finish the race.

The miraculous thing is that adventurers occasionally die in bed. Columbus survived three voyages, although some speculate that he died at age 54 of a rare tropical disease. Lewis and Clark survived their multiyear journey although Lewis caught something and the cure killed him. Clark lived for many years afterwards. But many of the early explorers were not so lucky. Balboa was beheaded, La Salle and Hudson died due to mutinies and some natives did in Magellan.

If you are born with the itch to explore, however, you aren't likely to be stopped by that fact that the trip might be dangerous. You just do it. Some guys even seek out danger, due to the way their brains work or don't work. They get a high from entering unknown territory—the kitchen, for example where sharp knives, pointy forks and meat grinders lurk, grinning like Mr. Death. It gives me nightmares thinking of the hazards ordinary Joes face—sometimes daily.

Women find the kitchen tame because their brains are better at controlling fine finger movements. Even out of the kitchen and home they are better able to consciously consider and weigh all the dangers ahead. If a woman starts into the unknown, she has made a good effort to turn it into the known—and has brought along travelers-checks, plastic, a wardrobe, gourmet food and designer water.

Besides the famous explorers and adventurers, there are ordinary guys who fill the pages of the Darwin Awards with their foolish and deadly escapades. And there are the lucky ones who sail oceans in small boats, climb mountains so high the oxygen molecules have to shout to be heard by their neighbors and dive to the deep ocean. Then, they return to tell us about it and we marvel or shake our heads in disbelief, wondering if we would have what it takes (mainly strength and stupidity) to leave our comfort zone behind and cross barren tundra with nothing but a compass, a snack and a Lear Jet.

Women adventurers do this too. I heard Helen Thayer speak about her adventure, a story detailed in her book *Polar Dream: The First Solo Expedition by a Woman and Her Dog to the Magnetic North Pole*. It required incredible strength and courage to do this trek alone with one dog to scare off an insistent polar bear, patiently looking for a meal. Such women remind us that there is a spectrum of capabilities in men and women. Although our focus is on average guys, we realize there are guys who would never set foot on an adventure except for the mad morning drive to the office and women who can't finish one adventure without planning the next one. But on average, we know men score higher on physical risk taking—leaping tall buildings in a single bound, for example, or wearing a wig, dress and nylons to the office Christmas party.

The thing, is guys are out there having adventures all the time—even at this very moment. Two guys are driving on a country road and one says to the other, "I wonder what it will do?" So, the driver steps on it and before you can say "crash victims" they zoom into the next county and then into the next world. Once there, they sit on deck chairs drinking Ambrosia Lite and repeating over and over, "Man that thing smoked, didn't it?"

I come by this skill honestly myself. Dad and Uncle Jack used to get the see-what-it-will-do urge with a speedboat they built. They would wait until the gas tank was nearly empty, remove anything not nailed down, including the kids, the engine cover, floorboards and life jackets and seek to set a new speed record. Once, a friend who was racing them decided to sit on his outboard motor to get more speed and fell off. That put a damper on the races for a day or two, until the friend thawed out. Did I forget to mention it was January?

Sometimes the goal of these efforts was to see if the boat would flip over if you ran it full speed and turned it so fast it swapped ends and headed the other way. Meanwhile, we kids watched and learned.

I do recall a couple military jet pilots who did the same end-swapping stunt over and over with their own boat. At last, one of them was thrown so hard from one side of the boat to the other that he broke three ribs, which hurt in spite of the pain killing effects of alcohol administered internally, since that's where the ribs are.

I was telling a friend about these two pilots and he topped my story. It seems an acquaintance of his was a navigator on B-52 bombers. He once flew with a daredevil pilot who liked to see what those lumbering behemoths would do. Apparently, they will do rolls and loops that should only be performed at air shows by stunt planes.

The acquaintance, suffering from a bad case of common sense, refused to fly again with the daredevil. Not so some visiting generals. The daredevil took off and was so anxious to show his elite passengers what a B52 could do he rolled the plane before gaining enough altitude—creating a momentary lineup at the pearly gates where St. Peter, guy that he is, gave everyone a free pass to the big hangar in the sky.

> The Constitution gives every American the right to make a damn fool of himself.
>
> —John Ciardi

In case you hadn't noticed, this is the downside of adventurous guys—they try too hard to have fun and end up paying the ultimate price.

I'm tempted to advise guys not to have any further adventures. Yet, when you read stories of successful adventures, you are amazed and your spirits are raised because you see what can be accomplished in spite of impossible odds. There's something in the human spirit that longs for adventure. We have to find what that is and eradicate it like ants in the pantry.

Until then, wrong guys will continue to pursue adventure. The cause might be testosterwrong, other chemicals out of whack or fear of boredom. Whatever it is, it isn't going away quick enough to keep men and women safe at home where they belong.

So, all we can say is good luck, and when you get back from your latest adventure, send us your wrong stories.

It's always more pleasant to read about amazing adventures where the subjects survived, like Shackleford's failed attempt to reach Antarctica. The amazing adventurer brought all his men home alive, in spite of ridiculous odds. The story is dramatized in a documentary (and a book by Caroline Alexander) called not surprisingly *The Endurance*. The name came from the doomed ship the men took south. Would that all adventurers were equally successful at failing to reach their goal but succeeding at returning home alive. Viewing failure as success is wrong, and we highly commend wrong to all, especially when it includes survival.

Closer to home, I recall a small adventure of a neighbor on Super Bowl Sunday. He had some friends over for the game and realized they were running low on brew. Not wanting to drive his car and risk having an accident or getting a ticket, he did a quick survey of the garage and heard the call of the riding lawn mower. He drove it out of the garage, down the sidewalk and across one teeny tiny street to the store parking lot, keeping well away from any traffic.

He was a model of caution, for a guy who considered himself too drunk to drive. He bought the required amount of beer, loaded it on the grass catcher and was nearly across that annoying street when the policeman stopped him. Apparently, the riding lawnmower was not street legal, among other things. At least the man learned his lesson, namely there is danger in the naked city and great or at least tale-worthy adventures can be had around any corner.

We owe a great deal to the spirit of adventure that lives to some extent in all of us. You might be living with an adventurer in your house. We suggest you get plenty of insurance. Then relax and enjoy the stories for as long as they last.

We will likely be collecting stories of guys just doing some adventure as we wander the halls of the nursing home with our emergency beeper going off, because we just stood up on our broken leg and went clunking down the hallway in our cast—leaving wheelchair and nurses far behind. It's not always pretty being a guy, but it can be pretty amazing.

It isn't something guys control either. We are heroes the way those penguins are heroes for bearing their young in the impossibly cold artic. The females heroically produce eggs and the males heroically care for them for months without food. A guy who sets his mind to a task is similarly single-minded, not simpleminded, as critics of guys suppose.

We think of Wrong Bob and the spring day he had to get to the airport, after dropping daughter Laura at school. Bob's wife Alayne was already at work. Meanwhile, a snowplow had passed, making the street sweet to drive on, as long as you could climb the mountain range of snow blocking the driveway. After the requisite three tries to tunnel through the mountain, Bob knew he had to choose another option. Being a guy, it didn't occur to him to call school and tell them Laura was taking a personal snow day. He knew there must be another way, a guy way, full of charging forth and defeating the villainous weather.

His house sat on a newly developed block and no fences had yet been built. Bob saw an opening and took it, cutting across his lawn to the backyard. Then, he entered the land of wrong, knifing through two neighbors' yards and leaving a deep trench in freshly planted grass on a recently built and sold house. How sweet the success of breaking through to pavement one block over from his vicious driveway and heading to school with Laura. But the story didn't end there.

Many roads were icy, in spite of the efforts of snow removal equipment. Bob dropped Laura at school and headed for the airport, worried he would be late. He braked at the bottom of the first hill, slid across the street and slammed one front wheel into a curb, flattening the tire.

Undaunted, he banged his knuckles trying to pry the hubcap off and changed the tire—putting only a small hole in the knee of his dress slacks. He made it to the airport in time to discover that his meeting had been moved to a different city, and the new flight didn't leave for several hours, time enough to buy new pants, check the phone book for landscape repairmen and set up an appointment for a wheel alignment, since the car now moseyed down the road at an odd angle.

Wrong Jim was giving away a sofa. If he were not a guy, he might have arranged for someone to help him move it three flights down to a trailer. Instead, he marched upstairs, pulled the sofa out of a storage room, paused to restart his pacemaker, slid the sofa down carpeted steps to the entryway and loaded it on a dolly. The dolly did most of the work on the way to an elevator. It didn't fit, but in the process of proving the obvious, Jim scraped a hole in the fabric.

A day later, after wife, Pat, had done her best to repair the damage, Jim resorted to asking a neighbor for help. Fortunately, Pat refrained from reminding Jim that had he only asked for help to begin with, the sofa would still be in great shape. Jim was a bit annoyed by this as he had prepared an excellent speech, the gist of which that she was giving away his favorite sofa. As a result, he had intentionally damaged it so parting would not be so difficult. Alas, the sofa left and with it Jim's fond memories of sleeping on it through chips, salsa, and Monday Night Football.

Not So Wrong Research Results

- Men have less of the so-called nanny neurotransmitter, serotonin (seer-otonin in wrong theory) and fewer receptors for it. This makes it easier for guys to act first, think later.

- Men have more dopamine (dope-amine in wrong theory) the so-called motivator neurotransmitter that intensifies effects of endorphins or natural opiates— producing a rush when men take risks.

- Result: We guys can get a natural high by doing the dumb things we do without thinking. Problem: it gets harder to get naturally high in that body cast.

- An enzyme monoamine oxidase, or MAO, is used to measure serotonin. High MAO equals a loudmouth nanny; low MAO equals a soft-spoken nanny. Low MAO equals high-risk taking. Professor Marvin Zuckerman says "there is no question there is a relationship between sensation seeking and platelet MAO." We say, "He's not only a Marvin, he's a Zuckerman!"

- Women and men don't vary in seeking new sensations and experiences, but men are more involved in thrill and adventure seeking through physically dangerous (that is, stupid) sports.

- Men are more given to losing control, which makes them useful in situations where you need lots of guys from the stands to rush onto the football field and eat dirt or break something.

- Men are more intolerant of boredom, which is why we cut this science stuff to half its original size and by the time you read this it will be the size of a postage stamp!

Based loosely on *Why Men Don't Iron* by Ann and Bill Moir (1999).

 **More Research Stuff**

- If seer-otonin serves as the brakes and dope-amine as the accelerator, guys like to step on the gas and check the brakes while crashing.

- Guys can build a tolerance to dope-amine and require greater and greater risks to get high—or dead, which some claim is less fun than high, but how else can you win a Darwin Award?

- A higher testosterone (T) level increases the dope-amine effect. Men who have the highest base-rate testosterone levels are the most aggressive—like Darwin Award winners. Medium T levels make for competitive men who have their hostility under control—like trial lawyers. Low to moderate level testosterone in men means better performance on spatial tests and ability to concentrate on a problem—like engineers.

- T levels vary with activities. If a man is about to start a race, his T levels can rise by forty percent, while women's levels do not change.

- Success raises the T levels higher, failure produces cortisol, which provokes anxiety—flight rather than fight. This may be why failure is no fun and success is very popular.

- Adrenaline controls the fear, fight or flight reaction. The more adrenaline released the better men do in competition.

- In summary, a bunch of chemicals mixed together inside our bodies are doing stuff without our permission. Once Congress gets out of jail, they should do something to put a stop to chemistry and maybe biology.

Loosely based on *Why Men Don't Iron* by Ann and Bill Moir (1999).

Feeling Wrong

I've saved up my complaints for a week. The coffee was cold on Monday and Saturday. On Tuesday, there was no salt on the table. You forgot to warm my slippers last night and you got lipstick on my cheek when you kissed me goodbye on Friday. Pass the sugar please.

Scientist Simon Baron-Cohen argues that the average man is good at systems, the average woman at empathy. The thing is, he doesn't just argue, he backs up his theories with data, which is wrong, wrong, wrong! For those who love to argue more than they love to know, it is disappointing to find that there is one answer to any question.

Science keeps taking away these areas rich in controversy. Fortunately, scientists will be figuring out men and women for another microsecond, so if you are a wrong husband, feel free to think you know what makes your wife tick. Since watches tick and wives talk, you are wrong and overconfident, in short, a perfect guy!

Another reason not to worry about science figuring out everything about women is that more than half of the scientists are guys and don't even know what questions to ask.

Then, there are books by scientists like Joseph LeDoux (The Emotional Brain: The Mysterious Underpinnings of Emotional Life 1996), which show the limits on our ability to understand ourselves. Where Freud talked about the unconscious, today scientists are mapping its mechanisms.

> ...wrong is bigger than guys, but we are waiting for more studies to prove it before we tell our wives they are idiots like us.

Life had a few ideas about how to survive and designed these into living things without them having to be conscious. Just because you are conscious, doesn't mean you know what you are doing—your unconscious brain and mind and body mechanisms are working away to keep your systems surviving and functioning.

Since these systems don't ask your permission to do their thing and since you aren't aware of what they are doing, conflicts can arise within as well as between spouses that they can't explain. This suggests that wrong is bigger than guys, but we are waiting for more studies to prove it before we tell our wives they are idiots like us.

Anyway, few of us are convinced by scientific studies—for one thing, we are only halfway through the comics, the snack bowl needs to be refilled and the game is on TV. Who has time to tune in NOVA? Not only do we ignore science at times, the best science seems to open new windows on our ignorance. Every study concludes that more studies are needed. The day more studies aren't needed, millions of scientists will be out of work.

Another problem with studies is this: they produce averages. We learn that women use both sides of their brains more than men, whose brains seem more specialized, but we also learn that individual men can have the female brain pattern and individual women the male pattern. If we don't ignore such complexity, it's like not knowing anything. But enough is known to let carelessly wrong guys speculate that the reason they are the way they are is because testosterone did a number on their brains in the womb as well as out of it.

Also, we can imagine that we will know much more about ourselves and rats in a hundred years or so, by which time we plan to issue a new edition of this book—the right edition. You might want to stop reading right here and wait for that one.

So, you didn't take my advice and you are sticking with the wrong edition of this book. Enjoy it. Meanwhile, husbands and wives will have to get along the same way we always have: Wives should continue to give husbands advice and husbands should continue to follow it—once all other options are exhausted.

Why husbands can't listen to begin with has to do with the need for counselors, police officers and bartenders to make a living. Clearly, a man's ability to not listen is an adaptation that helped the human race to survive until now. It is likely to destroy us in the next week or so, unless you wives out there patiently remind us of what you told us and we didn't listen to but need to know right now. Please!

I don't think we are wrong about this one. We have a real need to know whether cleaning the ceramic stove top with a razor blade scraper is a bad idea or not. This is important! Divorce court is overloaded as it is.

About Systemizing

- In a system there is an input, an operation and an output. If I push the red button, the projector advances to the next slide.

- Systemizing needs an eye for detail to discover the rules or laws. If I spin the baseball, it will curve.

- Even at one year, boys preferred to watch a video of cars over a talking head with the sound off; girls liked the talking head. Therefore, if the President was a dragster, guys would vote for it.

- At two, boys show stronger interest in cars and building blocks, girls in dolls, jewelry and adornment. Well, duh?

- In math, the same teachers teach calculation, where girls excel, and problem solving, where boys excel. This is true worldwide. We are still checking other worlds.

- In maps, boys tend to emphasize directions, routes or roads, where girls tend to emphasize landmarks. Then, the dog moves to the next fire hydrant and goodbye landmark.

- Boys are better at building a 3-D structure with Legos from a picture showing the front view. This is because they do spatial rotation of the teacher's answer book.

- Men are more accurate in Frisbee and dart throwing. They also are good at throwing Frisbees at darts and darts at Frisbees—until someone explains the rules.

- In 122 societies studied, weapon making is an all-male activity in 121 of these. In the other society, the major weapon is thought to be the cream pie.

See *The Essential Difference* by Simon Baron-Cohen (2003).

The Far Reaches of Systemizing

If Baron-Cohen is right and autism is at the far end of the male brain type, which is so good at systems, so what? He tells us, "People with autism…love to predict and control the world."

Well, wouldn't we all (or am I revealing my gender here)? But normal types recognize that the world is big and we are gnat-like compared to King Kong, the root system connecting aspen groves and the cream cheese that makes up the moon and several of the planets. How can we predict what a spouse or King Kong or all that cream cheese will do next? You think I'm being ridiculous about the cream cheese, but don't forget what the Pillsbury Doughboy did in the movie Ghostbusters. Would you have predicted it? I think not.

> How can we predict what a spouse or King Kong or all that cream cheese will do next? You think I'm being ridiculous about the cream cheese, but don't forget what the Pillsbury Doughboy did in the movie Ghostbusters.

People with autism actually try to control the world. Not being stupid, they try to shrink that world to a size and shape that can be controlled. They are more inclined to play games or deal with computers where the rules are clearly defined and the results predictable—or boring to those whose brains are not so wired. There's an old Taoist saying, "Who can sit quietly while the dust settles?" An autistic person can and will no doubt notice how many particles of dust did the settling.

The simplest solution, if you want to control the world, is to eliminate or sharply confine interactions with people, who studies show are notoriously hard to predict and seldom have the consistency of cookie dough.

If someone with autism is involved with unpredictable people, they become "anxious and disinterested." To have a relationship with such a person according to Baron-Cohen is "to have a relationship on their terms only." Imagine living in a town with one road and it's a one way street—it can't be easy.

> Clearly, wives are open systems, unpredictable, surprising and fascinating—but controllable? No way!

Clearly, wives are open systems, unpredictable, surprising and fascinating—but controllable? No way!

Men seriously into control have found ways to run their wife's life—but we suspect it is emotionally and financially less rewarding than working as a prison warden.

At the other end of the spectrum are women and fewer men with incredible compassion and empathy. These people have not been studied. For one thing, they are busy working in the helping professions. I met one such woman at a writing conference, who was writing books on the grieving process. My family met another, this time a man, who worked with my aging Dad. Such people are great. The woman remarked to me when I explained these concepts of empathy and systemizing that her son-in-law was indeed clueless when it came to empathy. He could see that people thought he was cold and unsympathetic, and he tried to do what they expected, but he was only guessing, not feeling.

Still, by recognizing that our brains can be wired differently, our hope is that we can begin to enjoy each other more and see value in our differences. Of course, as wrong guys, the idea of admiring various examples of homo sapiens is like going to a car show and seeing all the different models, finishes and custom options available.

We don't need to own each model to be surprised by the glossy flames on the side of one, the sleek lines of another and the powerful engine of a third.

Baron-Cohen also describes Asperger Syndrome (AS). These people often are high functioning, but with some of the symptoms of autism, such as difficulties in communication and obsessive behaviors. These conditions can affect anyone, but they affect males far more than females (about 10 to 1) and leave them feeling much less and observing and systemizing much more.

Of course, as wrong guys, the idea of admiring various examples of homo sapiens is like going to a car show and seeing all the different models, finishes and custom options available.

Baron-Cohen mentions a five-year old who knew the owners of each car parked on a city street, what the parking permit number was and when the permit expired.

Guys with high functioning cases of autism or AS often find themselves becoming experts in something—learning every detail there is to know and often pushing the boundaries of knowledge in areas like mathematics or science.

Many more or less normal guys enjoy mastering some area of knowledge completely. They might take basketball or baseball statistics and learn every player on their favorite team or all the players in a league to enable them to make decisions about their fantasy football team. They might learn some aspect of investing or master computer programming or know intricacies of a sport like golf.

I recall an incident when my sons were growing up. In high school, the older one knew enough about basketball to pick the winner of the NCAA Tournament in an office pool at our local high school, where I was an English teacher. The miffed basketball coach complained to me, "What does he know about basketball?"

Being a high empathy guy, I didn't say, "Apparently, more than you." But my son had memorized Basketball Digest for a couple years, played the game at his school, read the sports pages and grasped hold of a strategy.

"Dad, you know there will be upsets, so you look for the hot teams," he said as he lay in front of the TV and somehow picked the winning team. Of course, once he had done that, all the previous choices were more or less automatic—a system was at work after all. He certainly humbled more experienced sports guys that year.

Many men take special interest in mastering some area of sports or science—often becoming an expert in some collection of facts that others may not care about at all. You might not know you are sitting next to a man who has memorized the airline or train schedules for the coming year—unless you suddenly need that information and ask. But there are guys who store all this stuff in their heads, while the rest of us scratch ours and wonder why.

You might be a guy if...

You wait until a woman says, "Oh, how sad," about your golf partner's broken wrist before you agree and add, "I wonder if he'd mind if I borrowed his new Ping driver until the cast comes off."

You cheer when the opposing team's quarterback is taken out of the game with a career ending injury and then weep when you learn he was negotiating to join your team.

You spend the money for the family vacation on do-it-yourself plumbing and flood the entire neighborhood.

You take it on yourself to design the kitchen for the new house, even though the only time you've been there is when you needed a cold beverage from the fridge.

You come home two hours late for your birthday dinner because you kept winning free drinks in a dice game with the bartender.

Your favorite runs down the ski hill have the word cliff in them, and a notice at the top reads, "Experts Only."

Your idea of relaxing at the beach is flying stunt kites until your arms fall off.

You crowd out little old ladies and cut off other guys—making a race out of the short drive from the church parking lot to your favorite breakfast spot.

You buy a mail order bride from Siberia as your sixth wife, thinking if she doesn't speak English, she can't complain that you don't communicate your feelings.

You sign up for a cruise then complain when she makes you use valuable couch potato time to decide on which port tours to include.

More Science Stuff

The relationship between pre-natal testosterone and empathy is not linear. If the T level is too high, a male's ability on the spatial rotation tests declines. For women, ability on spatial rotation tests increases linearly with testosterone levels (probably because they never have too much). Men in the low-normal range for pre-natal testosterone do best on systemizing tests involving math and spatial ability. Men with special conditions that cause very low testosterone levels are worse at systemizing. Welcome to my world I'm tempted to say, although I'm not sure that explains why my office is total chaos. It could just be because I'm so focused on finishing this chapter that I ignore everything else, like the piles of books I keep falling over—which would be typical wrong-guy behavior.

We all know the brain has two hemispheres. Part of the effect of testosterone is that males develop faster in the right hemisphere, which is generally where spatial skills are centered. Females show more brain activity on the left side, early on, which is central to language. Women also use both hemispheres for language, so that if they suffer a stroke in one hemisphere, they suffer less impact than males, since the other hemisphere can handle language or learn to do so. Men often have more difficulty with language if they suffer a left hemisphere stroke. They also have difficulty with language if you ask them to explain the stupid thing they just did wrong—but that's another story.

Further evidence of brain differences comes from a test where one hemisphere can be put to sleep and the other hemisphere's abilities can be tested. Women become less fluent no matter which side of the brain is put to sleep, men's fluency is only affected when the left hemisphere is put to sleep. Makes you wonder if some guys can do this to themselves—you know, go totally blank on the verbal side and live in the land of empty space—a land formerly thought to be available only to zoned-out athletes, mystics and people watching TV for twelve hours straight.

A clue to what type of brain we own and operate is always with those of us whose minds live somewhere near their bodies. Doreen Kimura measured groups according to which side of their body was larger. She found that men with a larger left side had better verbal skills, comparable to women. Women with a larger right side had spatial abilities closer to average males. She measured fingerprints to make the distinctions (see more in the next chapter). Generally, the left or right foot is also bigger and the left or right breast and ovary in women and testis in men. All we can add is more studies are definitely needed and more popcorn, chips and beer.

Women Have More Empathy

- A natural empathizer imagines what another might be feeling and avoids offending them. Wrong guys wonder why they bother.

- By four years of age, every story told by girls was people centered, half of boy's stories were. The rest of the time, boys were making engine noises like, "Vroom, vroom!"

- On day one, female infants look longer at faces, especially eyes. Male infants look more at inanimate objects. This suggests boys flunk empathy long before they can mispronounce it.

- Baby girls at one year show greater concern for others. By age three, young girls are ahead of boys in inferring what people might be thinking. If guys ever knew what women were thinking, they wouldn't be so wrong all the time.

- Women are more sensitive to facial expressions, tone of voice, non-verbal communication. Wrong guys are sensitive to head transplants—but only if it involves their head.

- Women value altruistic, reciprocal relationships. Men value power, politics, and competition. Wrong guys have heard about relationships, but are taking a wait-and-see attitude.

- Empathy is a brake on aggression. Both sexes show aggression—men physically, women indirectly through remarks, gossip or exclusion. Tell a wrong guy you won't go shopping with him and watch him cry.

- Men use language skills to show off their knowledge, women use language skills to build relationships. A wrong husband would love to hear about her concerns—as soon as he finishes listing engine specs for every Porsche ever built.

- There are 412 discrete human emotions. A good empathizer might recognize 50 shades of hostility. Wrong guys recognize emotion when it punches them in the face.

See *The Essential Difference* by Simon Baron-Cohen (2003).

Notes from the
Cup o' Wrong Café

SUPER
Extra Strong
Jet-Black Coffee

Why doesn't science study what we want to know?
We want some studies of the big questions.

Why are more women nurses and more men emergency workers?

Why do women have hairdos and men haircuts?

Why do men pick their noses, butts, and scabs, and women pick lint from clothing?

Why do guys jump off cliffs and fear relationships?

Why do guys paint team colors on their faces more than women?

Why do we take women in pants seriously but laugh at men in dresses?

Why do women jump into relationships and fear cliffs?

Why do men shave their faces and women their legs.

Why do men show butt cracks and women show cleavage?

Bulletin Board Snippets

Why are bouncers men and receptionists women?

Why can physically weak women control stronger men?

Why do women wear lipstick but not men?

Why do men enjoy solving problems and women enjoy talking about them?

Why do we elect women to congress and men president?

Why do men wear suits and women outfits?

If a guy is alone in the woods with no women for fifty miles, can he still be wrong?

Wrong Genes and Biology

So a man has mapped the genome. A man? Like Andy? But
he never even asks for directions!

Every now and then The Theory of Wrong inventors
like to lean on the scientists and see if they fall over and hurt
themselves—including genetic researchers.

You will recall if you've looked at your genetic code lately
(it's usually kept under old tax returns in the attic), that 23
chromosomes come from Mom and 23 from Pop. Guys get an
X and a Y, while women get XX at position 23.

Some women only get an X from Mom or an X from Pop.
This is called Turner's syndrome. The odd thing is that those
who get an X from Dad have better social skills than those
who get the X from Mom. Turns out guys are carriers of the
very social skills they don't have.

Believe it or else?

- In women, language and spatial abilities are controlled by both sides of the brain. The corpus callosum which links the two hemispheres of the brain is larger in women. As guys, all we can say is this isn't fair.

- Men use the right side for spatial skills and the left side for language. It is easier for a man to talk and read a map because these activities are controlled independently.

- Women are superior in many verbal tests, which allows them to talk a guy into marriage before he knows it will be good for him.

- Women are more skilled in recognizing emotion sent to either brain hemisphere. Men are best at recognizing emotion transmitted to the right side—for example, when a girl slaps his right cheek.

- Women are less able to separate emotion and reason, but they are better at separating egg yokes from whites. We are still thinking about what this means to the chickens.

- Men have more difficulty communicating feelings because they use different sides of the brain for emotion and language. They don't know how to say what they feel, so please stop asking.

Various sources such as Simon Baron-Cohen, Doreen Kimura, Ann and Bill Moir and Leonard Sax. This is my wrong way of giving credit while trying to cover up my ingornance about who said what. I'm sure I didn't make this stuff up!

Normal women, with their XX genetics, have an advantage. They get a grandmother from each side of the family to tell them how to get along with two different families—which is the same as saying with everyone on earth. You can picture these two gray-haired ladies having conversations in the heads of women and pointing them in the right direction. One sits in a rocker on a porch facing the street and the other sits across the street. Using an elaborate system of hand signals and note passing—they stick the notes in the collars of neighborhood pets and send them back and forth across the street—they give women lots of advice on getting along in the neighborhood.

Meanwhile, in men's brains, there is one grandmother facing the same street. Across the street is Grandpa John, who is out in the garage, running power tools and making sawdust when he isn't checking the beer supply in the fridge. Grandma writes her notes and sends them across the street with Fido, but Grandpa shoos him away so he won't dodo on the lawn.

> The majority of husbands remind me of an orangutan trying to play the violin.
>
> —Balzac

The result is that if you are a guy, you really need to listen to your wife in order to complete the conversation between the grandmothers in her head and the grandmother in your head, who is getting so frustrated at being ignored she gives you headaches. (And you thought the headaches were from mixing rum drinks with straight shots of Tequila.)

The point is that when it comes to human relationships men are a grandmother shy of carrying on a conversation in their head about how they should feel about the kid in line who just skinned his knee and had to leave—and whether to accidentally trip and shove the next kid so he will skin his knee too. Guys lack empathy. But there's a reason for this or several reasons. One reason is efficiency. Look inside a frog sometime. You can do this on a web site. What you see is no empty spaces. Biology abhors a vacuum, which is why the woods are so messy.

The point is that if women and men were both good at the same things, they would compete with each other. Instead they complement each other. One is good at networking and empathy, the other is good at ignoring his own pain and that of others so he can beat an enemy, hunt mammoths and pull the ax out of his foot when it slips off the wood he was chopping. Empathy for the tiger at the door could lead to a crowded hut and a huge order of pizza.

Empathy Could Kill a Hero

Let me demonstrate how zero empathy can be strength. Let's say The Terminator comes home after a hard day of terminating. It was tough work. He blew people to smithereens, shot them, garroted them, drove over them—did everything to them except talk to them about their feelings.

He finds Ms. Terminator in the kitchen. He says hello, gives her a peck on the cheek and sits down to watch Fox Sports Network. The smoke alarm goes off. Ms. Terminator has burned the biscuits. He has to terminate her on the spot. It's sad and he wipes one tear from his eye, then heads out to get some fast food and a new wife.

We descendents from villain rooter outers still struggle today with the amount of force to apply to domestic issues...

Unconscious Emotions?

Joseph LeDoux has discovered the pathways fear travels to the amygdale—a part of the brain that talks the body into sweating, tensing, and peeing one's pants.

He also found the connection between the amygdale and the temporal lobes, where thoughts about fears sometimes become conscious. Unfortunately, the conscious connections are dirt roads. The unconscious pathways are superhighways. So, a phobia might be hard to get over because much of what goes on is managed by our unconscious or rat brain. With therapy, we can nudge the amygdale into not getting so upset over the sight of a snake. But then some shock occurs and the rat response to snakes returns. We think he said that.

The amygdale can trigger a cascade of events in the body that are difficult to control consciously. Chemicals can be released into our bloodstream and impact our bodies the same way they impact voles. When an eagle or terrorist attacks, we freeze then run.

So, guys are not only wrong, they are unconsciously wrong—and not just when lying on the couch. Where science has largely ignored emotion until now, the possibility of incorporating knowledge of physical components of emotion is exciting to many. But we believe ignorance is bliss.

Ledoux cautions that the can of worms he and others have opened should be cleared up in a century or so. If you can't wait to resolve your emotional differences with a spouse, we suggest outbursts of shouts, tears, and insane laughter—although we could be a smidge wrong there. In any case, enjoy the next 100 years of dwindling ignorance.

Loosely based on an interview with Joseph Ledoux on the website www.edge.org. Also see his books, *The Emotional Brain* mentioned previously, and *The Synaptic Self: How Our Brains Become Who We Are* (2002).

The good news is that he has just shown us how the same lack of empathy that made him effective in rooting out villains (gee, I hope they were villains, he may have forgotten to ask them) seems less appropriate on the home front.

So it goes. We descendents from villain rooter outers still struggle today with the amount of force to apply to domestic issues like plumbing, carpentry and why she is spending so much time at the office, instead of coming home to work on the good old relationship.

Kermit the Frog once sang, "It's not easy being green." It's also not easy to live with a spouse when genetics and biology aim to help us survive— but seem less concerned with helping us get along.

It's not easy to live with a spouse when genetics and biology aim to help us survive— but seem less concerned with helping us get along.

A couple united can be awesome. She can use her networking skills to schedule a trip and find a place to stay with friends or relatives, bringing along towels and sheets to lighten the load of hospitality. He can read the map without turning it upside down.

The fact that these roles can sometimes be reversed tells us it's more complicated than that, but the point is, our differences not only attract, they complement each other—filling in gaps that make a couple or family stronger as they face wave after wave of challenges. Like a surfboard and a surfer (don't ask which is which—it's a nonsexist analogy) together they do a better job riding the waves than either could do on their own.

Many of the differences in male and female brains are shared by animals. Castrate a male rat at birth and add female hormones and you get a genetically male rat with female behavior. Give testosterone to the mother of female rats and the offspring show male behaviors of rough play and better spatial ability in running mazes—just like the guy rats. So, humans are not unique. Still, it's easy to imagine how networking skills were valuable for women and male skills at systemizing, tool making and defending were useful to males over the eons.

> Give testosterone to the mother of female rats and the offspring show male behaviors of rough play and better spatial ability in running mazes—just like the guy rats.

For example, women may have developed their networking skills under somewhat adverse conditions. After a hard day of raping and pillaging, caveman Brad brought home rapee Angelina and a few other wives and children to the home cave—where he explained to main wife Jennifer how lucky she was to have more hands available to make baskets for holding all the new stuff he had pillaged.

Angelina had to rely on her superior networking skills to get past the cold shoulder treatment that faced her initially and get to the point where she and Jennifer could laugh together at Brad behind his back. Simon Baron-Cohen argues that women did have to network better because they often left the tribe and went with a man to his tribe.

However that may be, science is revealing enough differences in the brain wiring of men and women to write a book, which is, I believe, what we are attempting here.

Fingerprints Do the Talking

Research by Doreen Kimura demonstrates that some things are decided in the womb rather than on the playground. By the fourth month in the womb, finger prints are set for life. In the print of thumb and little finger on each hand are clues to your brain type.

Men tend to have more ridges on right fingers, women on left fingers. Kimura found that right-greater folks were better at guy stuff—throwing at a target, mental rotation, math aptitude. Left-greater folks were better at girl stuff—perceptual speed (finding a's), recalling pictures of things with names, and fine motor skills. Interestingly, left-greater men did better on tests women excel at. Right greater women did better on tests that men excel at.

Kimura also found that men and women with the left larger pattern appeared to have greater communication between brain hemispheres—the female pattern. So, a few women have the male pattern brains and a few men have the female pattern brains. Of course, this is wrong.

We think this whole thing is unfortunate because it further confuses wrong guys about who they are and why they can't find a's—for example on the conduct part of their report card.

Meanwhile, if you want to check your right or left testis, breast, finger ridges or foot, you might get a little more insight into why you are good at language or good at target shooting.

If a woman and can hit the grocery cart with a frozen chicken from twenty yards, she might have a guy type brain. Then, she can be wrong—how lucky can one girl get?

See Doreen Kimura *Sex and Cognition*, MIT Press, (2000).

Growing up Wrong

If you believe, you can almost walk on muddy water.

The male brain is the result of careful manipulation of the default female brain by androids like R2D2 but smaller, according to an issue of Science Comics we think we read—but we might have only looked at the pictures.

During the first four months in the womb, these androids (some science-types call them androgens like testosterone—but what do they know?) divide the brain into two sections—one for throwing stuff and the other for making logical connections like All men are mortal, Socrates is a man, therefore, Socrates can belch and scratch himself in public.

Next, a boy is born. He is pretty much beyond help by this point, but in case he has some redeeming qualities, they are removed at puberty by the release of more androids, which shift his voice to low gear, sprout hair all over his face, and install the key to the family car in the right hand, where it remains until surgically removed after too many tickets and accidents.

Eventually, the boy grows up to be an accountant and to drive safely, but the interim between birth and the midlife crisis is enjoyable for those who like watching real-life bloopers and escapades.

Think of Tom Sawyer cleverly arranging for others to paint his fence by at first refusing to let them do something so fun. His may not have been an act of empathy, but it showed the ability of a guy to use his wits rather than his muscles. Nowadays, Tom would be on his way to management, which claims to do all sorts of things—using pay rather than fun as encouragement for the worker bees.

A few stories of guys growing up are collected here, but any family with the good fortune to have one or more boys could provide additional detail.

> ...the interim between birth and the mid-life crisis is enjoyable for those who like watching real-life bloopers and escapades.

Communicating Wrong

Wrong Jim was invited to an overnight gathering at a friend's house during his early teens. It was a wonderful house party, hosted by a family with a swimming pool.

Suddenly, the host mother came out of the house and hurried toward Jim. He had a phone call. It was Mom. All his friends had told their families that they were spending the night at this house. Not Jim. He lacked the kind of empathy that tells most people, parental units want to know where I am.

His parents requested that Jim learn to speak in more than mumbles after that. However, Wrong Jim didn't really get it, as he still wonders why his wife explains carefully to him exactly where she is going when she leaves the house and why she expects him to do the same.

He has learned to imitate her behavior without understanding it. This makes him a functional adult, however. Apparently, this communication thing is worth putting some effort into, even if it makes little sense to guys—especially guys who work in communications for a living and see it as a job. Don't you get a break from your job when at home?

Sledding into Trees

As a boy grows, he learns to listen carefully to his peers and follow them into the Land of Wrong—sometimes called the Land of Pain.

One day in Illinois, Wrong Bob headed past the simple sledding hills in his neighborhood to the most feared and terrifying hills of all—those in Krape Park. That's the park where hills are hills and boys are lumps in the snow—sometimes recovered during spring thaw.

Following his companions, Bob started down the most hazardous hill of all—Dentist's Dream, since it sent a lot of work their way. Accelerating, like a rock

> His sled was older and more set in its ways...it ricocheted off the very first tree—leaving a lump of Bob lying in the snow.

kicked off the edge of the Grand Canyon, Bob noticed how the other sleds negotiated the difficult swerves around trees that peppered the path to the bottom. His sled was older and more set in its ways: Where others swerved, it ricocheted off the very first tree—leaving a lump of Bob lying in the snow.

As his mother helped him out of the 67 layers of clothes required to brave the Illinois winter, she uncovered the point where the tree taught him a lesson. She let him rest until dinner. Bob never forgot his experience and learned that women have empathy. You don't get that from wrong guys. And empathy, like hot soup on a cold winter's day, is a comfort.

Keys to the Kingdom of Wrong

Wrong Bob grew in wisdom and in age, but not in that order. Finally he reached the age where he could cut himself with a razor and get a license to drive. For his sixteenth birthday, Wrong Dad gave Wrong Bob his very own key to the family car—so Bob could run all the family errands, keep the car full of gas and change the oil.

> Wrong Bob grew in wisdom and in age, but not in that order.

But this day was special. Dad offered Bob a chance to take a friend and drive to the County Fair! Bob called a few special friends, who biked or hiked over and admired the sleek lines of the family's station wagon and the practicality of vinyl seats covered with vinyl seat protectors, to keep the other vinyl looking new.

Our hero slipped the key into the ignition and the powerful V-8 engine roared to life. He slipped the transmission into reverse, stepped on the accelerator with a firm and youthful foot action and shot across the street into the neighbor's car. The beautiful drive was over in seconds.

A chastened Bob examined the damage. The neighbor's car looked pretty good dented, but what set it off from more humdrum vehicles was the chrome molding strip that curled out into the street like some eternal question mark about the meaning of life.

A strange thing happened, as he stiffened his quivery lip and told Dad. His Dad calmly asked if he had talked to the neighbors. Bob decided to keep breathing.

The neighbor was a square faced brick of a man named Louie. But Louie wasn't upset either. For one thing, it wasn't his car. It belonged to his brother—the Sheriff! Out of the shadows a dark figure loomed and darkened the entire living room, then squeezed out the door. "Let's take a look," said the Sheriff, in a voice that would startle thunder.

He took one step to the street and examined his dented car. Meanwhile, sweat poured off Bob. His stomach gurgled, his brain whirled. He wanted to run, but where? Thoughts bounced like fireballs too hot to handle.

> Out of the shadows a dark figure loomed and darkened the entire living room, then squeezed out the door.

Then a miracle happened. "Son, that's not so bad," said the Sheriff. "The Dent and Fix-It owner owes me a favor. I'll have him take care of it. You go and enjoy your birthday. I was sixteen once. Have a good time and be careful."

Bob learned another valuable lesson. Even tough guys can have empathy. Sometimes when it's least expected, they dish out something like kindness—but don't tell them that or try talking about feelings. As we've pointed out, guys can't talk about feelings, because the words for that inhabit a different neighborhood. While there is a connecting path, it's full of bats, cobwebs and dark corners. Don't go there.

Biking to the River

Wrong Jim grew up near a vicious river. In the spring it raged, in the summer it rocked and in the fall its whirlpools dug holes to China. Every year, someone drowned just thinking of stepping in that water.

Wrong Jim's Mom warned him and his brothers over and over, "Kids, DON'T EVER, EVER GO NEAR THE RIVER!" Since it was rare for her to speak in capital letters, the boys all listened.

> The engineer who develops a gizmo to shut guys' mouths at the precisely the right time will make a fortune.

In a summit meeting one day, they discussed their mother's message.

"I think she said don't go near the river," said one brother, putting Mom's message in lower case.

"I think she said don't fear the river," said a future lawyer among them.

"Then, Jim spoke. "She said don't go in the river."

"I can live with that," said the others. So it was. They went to the river on their bikes whenever they felt like it, but they never went in the river. This way, they could throw rocks, spit and roll boulders into the river.

Much later, at a family gathering, Mom said, "At least my boys never went near the river."

The boys should have known enough to let Mom have her innocence, but they blurted out together, "Huh? We went to the river all the time."

This brings us to another problem with guys. Sometimes they talk when they should shut up. Guys are mostly strong silent types. Those who talk at all can talk forever about oil changes and stereo equipment. But most guys do a John Wayne impression: few words, fewer thoughts. Every so often, however, they talk when they should John Wayne it. The engineer who develops a gizmo to shut guys' mouths at the right time will make a fortune.

Biking the Hills

Wrong Jim joined some friends in the pine covered hills near his childhood home. He was on his bike. So were his friends. They lived on their bikes. It made school a little tough, but they loved their bikes. His friends were teaching off-road riding in the tree covered hills.

Then he rode full- tilt down the hill.

They rode down a couple hills. Finally, it was Jim's turn to lead. He used his male spatial skills to examine the hill, picking the places where the trees were sparse and aiming for a thin spot in the brush at the bottom. Then he rode down full-tilt.

155

Right girls would have stayed on the road. Jim rode into the unknown and made a discovery. The bottom of the hill had a dry creek with a creek bank that instantly stopped Jim's front wheel.

Wrong Jim was launched onto rocks cushioned by prickly brush. That was the end of Jim's brief career in off-road biking.

Of course, modern men have gone far beyond this pale tale. Nowadays, bikes have shock absorbers to absorb something which might be termed shock. For example, one young man told us of a landing he did with his mountain bike that blew out all the shock absorbers on the wheels and the seat and inside the guy's brain.

That's guys for you—always pushing the limits in search of fun and adventure.

> Wrong Jim was launched onto rocks cushioned by prickly brush. That was the end of Jim's brief career in off-road biking.

Walking on Water

Son of Wrong Jim was out with his cousins exploring the woods, when suddenly a muddy stream jumped out in front of the boys, blocking the path home. The boys huddled for a strategy session.

One wanted to go the long way around the stream. Another thought they could build a bridge out of some downed limbs of trees. But among them was a boy of vision beyond his years.

"Look," said Scott. "It's not water; it's mud. I think if you run really fast you can make it."

> I think if you run really fast you can make it.

Certainly, this was a big thought and, while it might seem unworkable except for a boy with bionic legs, Scott put thought into action, raced across the stream and came home clean as a whistle. Or did he?

Another version of the story holds that three cousins showed up at the house, two laughing hysterically, while a third looked somewhat forlorn and drenched in mud from head to foot.

Still, the theory is sound. If you go fast enough, usually about 40 mph behind a boat, you can barefoot ski, so Scott was right in theory and wrong in practice.

Isn't that guys in a nutshell? We have visions of being heroes. But little things get in the way and we end up flat on our face and covered in mud. That's why in the Land of Wrong we keep plenty of fresh water, dry clothing and a welcoming hand out to others when they fall like we all do now and again.

Wrong Through the Ages

Ye Old Steak Place

No! Tell them not to flatten it! I like the menu.

The universe has been around a long time—at least as long as the Ms. and Mr. Universe contest.

Some say the earth is three or four billion years old—but many of the people who lived back then are old now and have suffered some dementia—so they might be wrong.

We wrong theorists hold that recorded history began with the first World Series of Baseball in 1903. Some think that's when life began. We aren't sure and are willing to listen to other viewpoints—sort of, when our male earplugs aren't in place.

Speaking of earplugs, I had my male blindfold on this Sunday when I went to breakfast with my wife (historical because it happened and you are reading about it). She got a table, while I parked the car and then searched her out, sat down and began slurping coffee in an annoying male fashion—annoying to everyone except the slurping male.

"Notice anything?" she finally asked.

I hadn't, but at her prompting I looked up and saw a new light over the table. However, that wasn't enough to satisfy her.

"Now, look around," she said to me, the kindergartner of observation.

I looked around. It was unbelievable. I failed to notice an entire change of décor. I used my right brain to focus on the spatial, nonverbal task of finding the wife, while ignoring anything that could be considered not-wife. So what if there were new tables, chairs, booths, lights, wall colors and carpeting—none of those items fit the description of wife. I didn't see them. Once I did, I was amazed at my own blindness. How did I do it? I don't know, but it didn't require conscious thought. Guys can do this—not think about anything—

> This remarkable ability of men to ignore details... enabled us to write the history of just about everything in a few pages.

much easier than girls. I'm not saying we are proud of this fact, but we are capable of zoning out words—the meat of that thing called thought.

This remarkable ability of men to ignore details and focus on a goal enabled us to write the history of just about everything in a few pages. This is going to save history students a lot of time! No really, don't thank us now. Wait until you finish the chapter.

The History of Everything

It took a long time, possibly millions of years for life to think about getting out of the ocean and oozing into downtown Manhattan during rush hour.

Meanwhile, we had to go through lots of biota, cockroaches, and platypuses before we arrived at the king of beasts—human beings.

Several years later, the Sumerians invented cuneiform writing and by the time they could read it, the Babylonians had taken over.

The rest of recorded history is pretty much the story of one tribe conquering another tribe. You can substitute any names you want and the result is the same: winners, losers and those grateful they lived left or right of the war zone.

> It took a long time, possibly millions of years for life to think about getting out of the ocean and oozing into downtown Manhattan during rush hour.

History repeats itself. That's one of the things wrong with history.

–Clarence Darrow

Gradually, the tribes became so large that cities had to be invented and walls around the cities. The walls were to prevent warriors from invading without knocking first. If you are an invader, we'd like to point out that it is rude to invade before breakfast. We'd like to point out some other things too, like we worked really hard to build up and if you tear down what we built up, you will just have to build up all over again, if your invasion succeeds. So, unless you are a friend of the building up industries, give some serious thought to invading very carefully—without breaking anything.

Back to our story of everything: We guys liked the cities and so did our wives, although they tended to tend the home fires, and we guys went out to explore and conquer more stuff. When we came back, the gates to the city were closed. This led to the greatest invention of all, the catapult—an invention still used today in some of our rural neighborhoods to launch old cars, toilets, and the occasional dead cow, which we find tasteless—not the cow itself, which properly prepared would taste like a hamburger—but the launching of it. Come to think of it, why doesn't cow taste like cow burger or beef burger instead of hamburger? This is something we intend to look up, once we finish the history of everything.

Soon, Alexander the Great conquered one place after another just to say that he could and then died young, and his empire fell apart. He didn't have much of a mind for business or profit, but he got a real kick out of conquering. Our theory is he never had a wife to love, cherish and obey, which worked against him babysitting the grandkids.

The lesson of Alexander is that if a guy's aggressiveness is not balanced by regular exercise and the love of a wife, he tends to smack down the walls of one or two city-states a day and sometimes by lunchtime. So, our advice to guys is to marry, and if you are married, stay that way. You will live longer, achieve greater success and have better lunches.

For example, when guys are more interested in impressing women than dominating other men, they put their energy into building Trump Towers or real architecture, instead of tearing things down and making huge messes—while thoughtlessly leaving no restaurants to enjoy a good meal at the end of a day of slaughtering and pillaging.

Women conquerors would have much more sense. They would check the menu of each restaurant before they knocked it flat. And wives of conquerors quite often remind the Alexander in their life that before they go off conquering and laying waste, they had better clean up the last mess they made.

> Women conquerors would have much more sense.

A few more things happened throughout history. For one thing, guys got really good at making empires like Greece and Rome. Rome became so powerful that a kind of peace settled over the world—although you might not notice, if you lived in the wrong neighborhood—but in general, we can say the Donald Trump model was more in vogue than the Attila the Hun model—that is until Attila the Hun came along.

Unlike Alexander, Attila had plenty of wives, who didn't stop him from ruthless conquering. This may be why he is known to have said, "Every Hun has a value—even if it is only to serve as a bad example." He was speaking of himself.

Supposedly, Attila was not much more barbaric than the age in which he lived, and he did move from the mere conquest model of Alexander to actual governing—so perhaps we owe that to those peace loving wives of his. At least, we know he was with a new wife when he died—of a nosebleed.

Attila was fond of saying, "Some Huns have solutions, for which there are no problems." However, this nosebleed was a problem with no solution. Fortunately, Attila died in pleasant surroundings for a guy without much empathy, and his empire was intact at his death, though not for long afterwards.

What's wrong with history so far is that it's so repetitive. The countries in power change, but they keep doing the same stuff. You wonder why we can't all get along. The reason is close at hand and it isn't only testosterwrong.

In *"The Trouble with Testosterone,"* scientist Robert Sapolsky points out that aggressive behavior produces more testosterone in a guy, rather than testosterone causing bad behavior. High testosterone—such as steroids produce—can make a difference, but only after an aggressive mood is already triggered.

What could possibly trigger that anger and aggression? Think locally. Surely, you can imagine someone you could smack once or twice and feel they deserved it. If you can't, you're not a guy or wrong.

Perhaps someday, confronted by an annoying jerk, you will smile instead of silently seethe or noisily smack them. This will signal a new age where history writers will chronicle World Networking I, and World Networking II instead of world wars.

These networking things will be massive events where we expend incredible capital to move our people over to talk to their people and their people over to talk to our people. .

Customs will be shared, ideas on food exchanged, a few of theirs will marry a few of ours. We'll be one happy family—with the problems happy families have, which tend to be the stuff of sitcoms rather than police dramas.

Actually, wars accomplish the same sort of networking but at a higher cost. They bring different cultures together and open our eyes and mouths to new foods—while teaching other cultures how to say "cheeseburger."

This is one positive purpose of aggression; it gets us outside our small enclaves or cultures or countries. Then, Achilles meets Helen and the rest is mythology or history with some romance and simple math thrown in—as in 1 + 1 = 2. Why everyone gets so worked up over a math problem that easy is beyond us—but then we inhabit the Land of Wrong.

> ...wars accomplish the same sort of networking but at higher cost...

Perhaps the most positive sign in the wrongness of history is that the population of the world has continued to rise. While this creates a great deal of pressure on resources, it also says we are doing some things right—for example giving pregnant women vitamin pills as big as their heads and eating fresh fruit to prevent the formation of stale fruit.

Still, we can't end this brief and grossly wrong history without mentioning the discovery in our own time of Rocky Road ice cream. Not only is it good to eat, the name pretty well sums up all of history—especially the parts where basalt, granite and guys are involved.

First Cup o' Wrong

"Look," said Eve, "I'll clean up your mess from poker with the parrots. You pick some cherries for a pie."

"Ok," said Adam. After a short walk he stopped confused by all the different fruit trees. "I wonder what a cherry is."

"You need some help?"

Adam was surprised Snake could speak English. Parrots were jabberers, but Snake? "I'm looking for cherries. Wife, Eve, wants to make a pie."

"I sold the last of them to the birds. I've got great apples." Snake slithered over to a nearby tree covered with red delicious."

"Aren't these forbidden? A voice told me to leave these alone."

"Rather wasteful, wouldn't you say? Try one."

"I don't think so. Not without checking with Eve."

The snake looked surprised, "And they talk about me being spineless. Maybe tough guys are more evolved than we thought."

"Wait," Adam flexed and took a bite. "I'll take a basket."

"Not so fast," said Lion. The trees probably talked too.

"Look, Lion," said snake, "no more until you pay up."

"Hold it! I could eat you both in one bite!" said Lion.

"I thought paradise meant never having to eat each other," said Adam.

"When you ate the apple paradise ended," said Lion.

"So you heard the voice too?"

"Sure, we all heard it."

"I don't have ears," said Snake. "Look, life's just getting started. Let's multiply first and eat each other later."

It sounded good. So Adam took apples home to Eve.

"I can't believe you didn't bring cherries. I only ask one little thing and you can't even do that right."

"Snake told me the birds got the cherries.

"Snake is trouble. You listen to him, pretty soon we'll be paying for food, and we'll all have jobs at Wal-Mart."

"Actually, he made me pay for the apples," said Adam. "And paradise is over, because we weren't supposed to eat these."

"That's it! After this, I'll get the fruit, you clean."

"Yes, dear," said Adam. "And I'll be careful not to break your obsidian bowl with the inlaid jade."

"Don't touch that bowl. Don't touch anything. I'll do it all."

"Yes, dear," said Adam, the joy of wrong spreading through his body like the warmth of a fire on a cold night in paradise lost.

Wrong History

Roman Equestrian Mundus loved Paulina so much he was ready to starve himself if he couldn't have her. But she was a faithful wife. Using bribes, his brilliantly bad serving girl, Ide, talked corrupt priests of Isis into convincing pious Paulina that a god wanted to sleep with her. Really! Mundus had his ungodly way with Paulina then bragged to her. Shocked, she told her husband who spoke to the emperor. He had the priests and Ide killed and exiled Mundus—very wrong, very male Mundus. Why this isn't a movie, I don't know. Josephus, *The Antiquities of the Jews: Book 18.3*.

Attila and Herod the Great had in common the wrong tendency to kill their own offspring—in Herod's case due to paranoid fears that they were out to get him, leading Emperor Augustus to say, "It is better to be Herod's dog than his son." This isn't funny, but dogs find it encouraging. Somehow, this makes me think of today's terrorist leaders turning their "brothers and sisters" into suicide bombers. I mean wouldn't you feel used? If you could still feel, that is.

Wrong Napoleon demonstrated how to win the battles and lose the war—losing more than ninety percent of his army in a foolhardy campaign into the teeth of the Russian winter. Later, the French gave him one more chance, and he made Waterloo famous. But don't forget, he has a dessert named after him.

Simon Baron-Cohen notes the cruel truth that the way to success in most primitive cultures is through murder, a sign that civilized behavior, such as gaining power by elections is an advance over a seeming black hole of rule by lethal force. Throughout the world, democracy rules in less than half of all countries. If democracy succeeds, perhaps it will be because dictators fall on the sword of the Internet. Information rules!

Collecting Wrong

Do you want to see my lifetime collection
of beer bottle labels?

There is a lot of hullabaloo about romance and it can fill
up a life if you let it. But most guys don't let it. Somewhere
in the primitive brain or spinal column—or possibly the little
toe—lives the past experience of the race and it calls out to
guys, "Collect stuff, collect stuff, collect stuff."

On a recent trip, Wrong Jim met one such fellow. He
resolved early on to never marry. At first Jim was surprised
that a man would be so wise or foolish (depending on your
viewpoint) even at a young age. Then, Jim learned that the
gentleman had a higher calling—collecting train sets and
modeling them.

Apparently, there is a big difference between mere collecting and modeling. Model trains are the ones you see at county fairs or at model railroad conferences. They look like landscapes that happen to have tiny trains as a prominent feature—along with small cars, buildings, trees and shrubs, and plastic people.

The only thing they generally lack is the model junkyards and warehouses that real trains seem to always pass as they enter towns and cities. That's because these wrong men are modeling a different era, when passenger trains were a bigger deal, and there were no junkyards because in that idyllic yesteryear all the cars ever created ran forever.

It was clearly an act of great foresight for this train modeler to know that a wife would not allow every room in the house except the bathroom and kitchen to be filled with model trains. She also might want gifts occasionally, new carpet now and then and a new car every million miles. Such frivolous expenses would drain his train budget needlessly, so the man stayed single and happy.

He was on his way to a model train convention and so were a few others on the real train Jim was riding. It may have been an odd group of collectors, but of four passengers going to this convention, one was married. He ran a family business creating and selling train cars to

> It was clearly an act of great foresight for this train modeler to know that a wife would not allow every room in the house except the bathroom and kitchen to be filled with model trains.

the others—the collector types, guys whose testosterwrong powered brains jettisoned empathy in the interest of housing masses of information about stuff in the brain area otherwise relegated to emotional connections with people.

They were all nice enough folks, these collectors, with the possible exception of the lawyer who drove one lady out of the parlor car with a dumb and sexist joke. No, the lawyer wasn't nice, but I overheard him brag that he had hardly ever lost a case. So one use for low empathy collectors of information is they can use incredibly detailed knowledge to win legal battles.

Clearly, some guys follow a genetic instruction to collect stuff. They learn every classic movie or rock song by heart, and then study the lives of each performer. They slurp up facts like pigs at a trough, organize them like a computer and spew them out until your eyes glaze over. Young guys learn Harry Potter backwards and forwards. Old guys learn genealogy.

Young guys learn Harry Potter backwards and forwards. Old guys learn genealogy.

They do it for the same reason people climb a mountain or sprawl on a couch—because it's there and it feels good to them. No doubt it feels good because it gives guys a sense of mastery, control and power. Collections also put guys in touch with the past and allow them to relive happy moments via collections that are timeless, eternal and good.

Wrong guys make expert collectors. It was a guy who kept winning Jeopardy for umptysquat days. It is guys who think of train spotting as a hobby. It is guys who sometimes get into fistfights over a seemingly safe activity like bird watching. ("You scared it away on purpose before I could see it and record it! Take that." POW! BAM! THUMP!) Collecting is not for the faint of heart or sensible of head.

Guys and gals come in all varieties: a spectrum from extreme male to extreme female. It is true that you see men and women collectors. Many women might use a collection primarily as a way of meeting and talking with other people. For example, scrap-booking is a popular thing for some women to do and they go to scrap-booking parties. At these parties, they share ideas and materials and no doubt gossip and show concern and caring for the less fortunate among them, who only have one scrapbook to their name. The scrapbooks are important to women but so is the networking.

"You scared it away on purpose before I could see it and record it! Take that." POW! BAM! THUMP!

For guys, the networking is important if it leads to a better collection. In competitive collecting of say stamps, sometimes only one guy can have the very best collection. There might be only one of a particular stamp. The competition thing works its way into the sport.

For women, not so much. They want a nice collection but each scrapbook is designed to tell a story—a story they would be happy to share with others along with the techniques they used to make it come together.

Guy's interest in stuff over people is the key reason for a difference here. There is a secret pleasure men get from knowing they have a complete collection of something. They don't need others to know, but their inner soul burns brighter for having these things.

There are some strange people and strange collections out there. One of the more unusual collections was by a certain unnamed male I heard about whose parents had to start him on the strange act of collecting nail trimmings. He had his lifetime collection and displayed it in a bowl. I'm sure someone else has all the hair ever cut off of their head. Hopefully, no one out there is collecting other material that departed their bodies, but don't bet against the collecting gene.

Of course science has led to unusual library collections. A national laboratory I worked at had participated in experiments with certain dogs to learn about radiation effects on mammals. The research ended, but a library of the dog organs exists. Not the sort of thing you display in your living room or even discuss in a book, unless you are a wrong guy. Then, there are the archaeologists, some of whom dig through modern dump sites to discover what modern man tosses away— just as they would sort through pottery shards, bones and other remains of ancient civilizations to try to understand life in other ages.

You can argue that scientific collections serve some purpose, but many of us collect things to collect things. We might wallpaper a wall with wine labels, or cover it with wine corks or bottle caps.

One folklore theory is that there are only two ways to organize a collection of stuff—vertically in vertical files, or horizontally in flat piles that soon become vertical towers. In reality there

You can argue that scientific collections serve some purpose, but many of us collect things to collect things.

are several other methods, such as the loose bin and the loose bin with the sides removed, sometimes referred to simply as chaos—which is the method we recommend.

Some men use all of these systems and a few more. On our travels into rural America, we have seen a bend in a river, which will remain unnamed (ok, it's the St. Joe River and the reason it is unnamed is because I'm afraid the owner of the shed will hurt me if he reads this).

There's this shed on an otherwise scenic river where you can see collecting gone crazy.

There's this shed on an otherwise scenic river where you can see collecting gone crazy: truck tires of various sizes stacked horizontally and vertically; machinery that might be useful if buggy whips come back in style; boxes of stuff that only a logger could love; saws and metal beams and arms and chains and nails and bolts and nuts; all of it clearly visible behind a collection of sinking docks and under the collapsing shed roof—a precarious pile of treasures for the tough guys standing on a timber platform today next to the shed and measuring something, as if they planned to renovate the place, although how you could improve on such perfection without a match or a bulldozer is hard to imagine.

Many, especially Martha Stewart's women, would be appalled to be associated with such dilapidation, such decay, such a disaster. However, there are men among us who looking at the same mess hear a question forming involuntarily inside our heads: "I wonder how much he wants for that set of backhoe tires? I could set them in the backyard and plant a tree in each one and they would make a set of benches for folks to sit around and watch the weeds grow while they drink some beer and eat some barbecue."

Such men have a knack for seeing diamonds where the rest of us see dust. So it is in many garages, backyards, side yards and even some front yards across this thriving country of collectors. Men collect valuable stamps in neat folders and piles of apparently worthless stuff that their sharp eyes see as useful and therefore beautiful.

> Such men have a knack for seeing diamonds where the rest of us see dust.

Men own coin collections worth thousands of dollars and beer bottle collections worth five cents a bottle in states that pay a redemption fee for glass bottles and nothing at all anywhere else.

Those really into their collections spend time with them, organizing records or songs or books by favorites or periods. They arrange the best blues albums of the sixties, the best bourbon bottles of the thirties and the best combines of the past century.

Yes, that last item is no typo. There are rich men who collect farm equipment. The one I was told about is no farmer. He simply likes farm equipment and keeps it shining and new in a huge warehouse. This is wrong, but it keeps farm equipment manufacturers and their employees busy and reduces the amount of money this man can spend on his gun collection, which is certainly more dangerous.

But I find the quirky collector of things that would otherwise be thrown away most loveable—because we live in a throwaway society and occasionally what gets tossed is one or more of us. How comforting to know someone is out there picking up old wrecks and damaged goods, whether human, animal or mineral with the intent of restoring and using it.

These geniuses of junk see value in things the rest of us toss aside without qualms. Their garages are overflowing with finds from garage sales, piles of things that were labeled free and set by the curb, things in the backs of trucks on the way to the dump. Such men see value everywhere—among the old, worn, broken and mended. To these clear-eyed visionaries everything is salvageable—even politicians and lawyers.

They salvage memories as well. An old enameled pot might be on a shelf because for years the camp cook used it during hunting season. A pickup that no longer runs only needs a new head gasket, some wheels and a door or two and it will be good as new.

And there are the deeper reasons why guys collect stuff: unfortunately, they are guys and can't tell you what those reasons are but let me try.

Hanging onto stuff for some of us is tantamount to hanging onto life itself with its memories and experiences. So, God protect us from renovators, developers and spring cleanings. It might be wrong to collect useless stuff, but value is always in the eye of the beholder. Just because more people agree on the value of diamonds or gold or Internet stocks doesn't mean that hubcaps or bottle caps or potato chips that look like Lincoln are unworthy. It takes all kinds to make

> Hanging onto stuff for some of us is tantamount to hanging onto life itself.

a mixed up world, a wrong world, the kind of world we have and probably the kind of world we wanted, even if we claimed and fervently believed we wanted something better.

In the final analysis, guys' ability to collect and organize the stuff of the universe is important and not to be taken lightly. Well, it can be taken lightly by people who value people more than stuff. But it isn't taken lightly by the collectors or those who suddenly need some information from a collection.

There is a divide that can't always be bridged between valuing people first and stuff second and the other way round. Perhaps our train modeler was right to never marry—thus saving one household from endless arguments.

And it can be difficult for those who connect empathetically to others to eventually learn that a mate relates better to his toys than his family.

The world isn't fair, but it's fun—as long as we can appreciate wrong guys without expecting too much. Yes, once they read this book, wrong guys may admit to being wrong guys. It's a step. We will have to be reminded several times why we are wrong and what we should do to change—if that were even possible.

> There is a divide that can't always be bridged between valuing people first and stuff second and the other way round.

The best alternative for right mates might be to seek opportunities to connect with their wrong guy. Honor his abilities in collecting detailed facts about stuff when you can. Use him as your key source of information about life issues—like whether the concrete in Grand Coulee Dam is enough to build Saks Fifth Avenue stores in every city of the world, or only in the 48 contiguous states, two noncontiguous states, Puerto Rico and Guam.* Guys know this stuff cold.

*The answer is every city of the world, if they leave out the men's department.

Wrong for Life

Guys! Measure your progress in the Land of Wrong!

Hugs & Kisses

Cook Dinner

Stuck Your Foot In It!

Blew It Big Time!

Hey! I'm a Guy

A Night Out

Teeny-Weeny Bit Wrong

You Did It Now Buddy!

THE ORIGINA

WRONG-O-METER

Cruise for Her

Dead Wrong

Mucho Wrongo

Chocolate

Earned Your Black Belt in Wrong

Way, Way, Way Wrong

Jewelry

Flowers

THE
Wrong-O-Meter
The original, accept no substitutes.

Guys! Have your wife adjust the patent-pending Wrong-O-Meter scale to see just how wrong you are, then check our handy dandy list of actions to take to move back to OK. You'll love our Wrong-O-Meter and your wife will love you as she watches you move the Wrong-O-Meter to Almost Right before her very eyes.

If you've stayed with us this long, we are proud of you. If you flipped ahead and found this page by accident, you're one of us—living proudly in the Land of Wrong without knowing all the stuff that would get you out of your latest wrong adventure with only minor scrapes and scratches.

We've simplified the lessons of wrong in this chapter so even we can understand them.

Not to worry. We've simplified the lessons of wrong in this chapter so even we can understand them. We started this book as a lark, without much thought of what it would be about or how it would help mankind meet and greet womankind without falling into the hole called unkind and breaking an ankle.

Now, in occasional lucid moments, we can glimpse ways this Theory of Wrong stuff could actually help us guys get a free pass to a fun roller coaster ride called life with a wife. So, let's get on with it because time's a-wasting and if we stand on the track much longer the roller coaster our wife is on is going to smack us silly.

This brings us to Lessons in Wrong, but before we get there, let's pause a moment to reflect on the beautiful gift of wrong we offer each one of you. It's on the cover and in black and white at the beginning of this chapter. I'm speaking of course of the patent-pending **Wrong-O-Meter.**

While our theory holds that wrongness is a natural state for guys and women shouldn't expect anything else, occasionally we have to pay the price for being guys and letting women do most of the heavy lifting.

So, we thought we would explain the Wrong-O-Meter once and for all. Actually, this is not only The Original Wrong-O-Meter, it is the primitive Wrong-O-Meter. A more advanced model has a window as well as an arrow on it, so you can spin the dial and see detailed actions to take to have her begging you to don your black belt in wrong and head for whatever husband heaven suits you best.

The key point is you live your entire life in various stages of wrong.

Unfortunately, our wives won't let us release this version just yet. Too dangerous, they say. So, we are stuck with the published version, which is pretty self-explanatory. The key point is you live your entire life in various stages of wrong. You always are in debt to the woman in your life who continues to bail you out of relationship jail. But sometimes guys, you are only a teeny-weeny bit wrong and life is good.

Then, there are the times when you earn a black belt in wrong. Life is good then too and that is the segment of the meter next to Dead Wrong—the worst wrong of all. This means life is good most

Dead Wrong is not so good.

of the time, even if you are wrong. Dead Wrong is not so good. You are stuck at home while she goes off on a cruise with her girlfriends at best and at worst in search of some guy who will not be wrong all the time. Since this is impossible to find, why worry? Sooner or later, she will realize the truth that all men are wrong and give up men entirely or return home and give you another chance.

This time, do wrong right for once, ok? You are giving wrong guys a bad name.

Lessons in Wrong

1. People are fun to watch.

2. Women and men complement each other.

3. Get two tubes of toothpaste.

4. Let the kick under the table be your guide.

5. Create his space and her space.

6. Polish your prize.

7. Even a genius is an idiot at home.

8. Give wrong a chance.

9. What to do when wrong is not enough.

People are fun to watch

Why would you want to live in the Land of Wrong when you could inhabit the Land of Right? Let me tell you, the Land of Wrong has more smiling people in it. Smiling releases chemicals in the brain that make you happy. You don't have to be happy to smile, but if you keep at it, you can't stay unhappy or angry.

Now get involved in a competitive sport with some guys. Watch the guy miss a shot and throw his club. Smile. You compete best when you are relaxed and loose.

Take the same attitude into the home. If your wife does something that annoys you, a relaxed state of mind will help you let go of your sense that there is only one right answer.

Then too, you smile a lot because you are enjoying watching yourself, your wife and those you meet as they negotiate life's paths. You open yourself to learning from those smooth operators that slide through life like it was a snow covered bunny hill. And you are amazed at others who turn the same hill into brutal moguls. You recognize that they are in the Land of Wrong and that's ok, but they don't need to stay there forever.

Women and men complement each other

Science, sitcoms and common sense tell us that men and women look, think and act differently. Each sex has its own biological advantages and together, acting as a unit, a married couple is stronger than either one is alone. The Theory of Wrong is one way for dominant and dismissive males to open themselves to their wife's unique and valuable viewpoint.

First quiet the mouth and remove the foot. It would be nice if the foot never entered the mouth, but in our experience, that's not the way it works. Take a break from the burden of being right and enjoy what the two of you can cook up together in the Land of Wrong.

Get two tubes of toothpaste

Life's eternal questions include the debate whether to squeeze from the middle of the tube or the bottom. Other questions like this include which way to install toilet paper, and whether to buy or lease underwear. The correct answers are: buy two tubes of toothpaste and manage your own tube; the person who installs the toilet paper gets to decide; and rent to own underwear.

Marriages sometimes fall apart over little stuff where the right answer is whatever works, not what is carved in stone or written in the genetic code. But people get highly exercised over the right way to do stuff, whether it matters or not. In the olden days, when toothpaste came in lead tubes, everyone was brain damaged, so it didn't matter where you squeezed.

It's never hard to argue, but it's often wrong to argue—unless the two of you enjoy the tennis match aspects of arguing and the chance to make amends afterwards in the bedroom—except when that's what started the fight.

Let the kick under the table be your guide

You've been there. It's election year. You have entered into one of the forbidden areas of discussion—politics—the other forbidden topic being religion.

You are with some people who agree with you and some who don't. Generously, you are letting the guys who don't agree learn from the great insights you have gathered. Soon, no one is listening, the decibels are rising and you feel it—the nudge under the table. We Theory of Wrong guys are here to tell you to pay attention to the nudge.

The nudge knows. Trust the nudge. She can get you out of the Land of Wrong quicker and easier than the formal apologies you will issue later, if you ever want to see these people again.

Create his space and her space

A garage, basement, or attic often can provide a space where guy-rules apply. This is wrong but good. The wife also benefits when she has a space to do her favorite hobby.

Often, it takes a moment away from the battlefield for the male to recognize the Land of Wrong. Then, it takes another moment to take off the armor of battle and wipe the sweat from his brow. Maybe after a few more moments, he can change a losing situation into a cooperative situation. That is real progress for a warrior.

Polish your prize

You won her heart at some point in the past, but you really don't deserve her. With your reduced empathy, you will never be able to feel what she feels and appreciate how she navigates the communication shoals and finds the channel to clear sailing over and over again. Give her a reward.

If you have the money, it might be jewelry or flowers. If you don't have the money, it still might be jewelry or flowers but in economical form. Polish the prize you won but don't really deserve.

Even a genius is an idiot at home

Einstein wasn't the best husband. He wasn't considered a genius of interpersonal relationships. When he entered the house, he had less chance than you have of being right. Keep this in mind. Einstein was smarter than Dale Carnegie, the author of *How to Win Friends and Influence People*, a contemporary of Einstein. But Dale was better with people.

We've referred to Donald Trump several times. He is certainly considered a great success in business and real estate. Yet he's been married several times. In a sense, the same Donald who fires people on *The Apprentice* has been fired on the home front multiple times.

The Theory of Wrong may not be right, but it might help you extend your relationship with your current wife and enjoy it. The other day Wrong Bob reported this story which shows what we mean. He was working on a project for his wife's framing business, which Alayne operates out of her home. This was guy stuff—putting long pieces of pipe along a wall that would store and protect framing material. Both mates viewed themselves in charge: Alayne because it is her business, Wrong Bob because he is used to running projects and this looked like a technical project a guy could handle.

But using the Theory of Wrong, Right Bob, the guy who manages multimillion dollar projects, stepped away for a huddle with Wrong Bob, the guy who can fumble a relationship move without even trying. Wrong Bob told Right Bob to back off until Monday, when he would be back at work and ready to rock and roll on his work. Then in a wrong frame of mind, Wrong Bob approached Alayne and asked what he should do next. Suddenly, the home front effort smoothed out and the frame shop owner rightfully got her way.

If the Theory of Wrong can help Wrong Bob deal with his wife, it can make your life better too. If it doesn't, you still end up with stories of wrong to enter in our contests and possibly win a fine wrong prize.

Give wrong a chance

All your life, you've been trying to be right, to win and to stay in front of the competition. Your relationship isn't a competition. You don't have to be right with a wife, you have to be honest, humble and flexible.

You have to listen, which you aren't used to doing, if you are anything like us. You shift gears in your car. Remember to shift mental gears when you enter the house. You don't have to win this one. You do have to admire her ability at empathy and honor it and let her lead in that department.

When you enter the Land of Wrong, you may not even know you've crossed the line for a time. But you will, and the quicker you see it and admit it, the faster the smiles spread and the joy of wrong reigns over all.

Sometimes, a slip of the tongue makes it easy to admit you are in the Land of Wrong. Wrong Bob had an occasion to lecture his two daughters. Mid-lecture, at a critical point he actually said, "When I was a little girl..." Result: Lecture over as the family, including Bob, rolled on the floor with laughter.

What to do when wrong is not enough

As we've mentioned elsewhere, a quick and simple admission of wrong when you buy her an extension cord for her birthday may be a major step for a guy—but it might not be enough for your mate.

Several women have complained to us that we are wrong about women. This pleased us initially, since it seemed they got the point we were making. But on further consideration of the rotten tomatoes tossed our way, we are ready to admit that just like in the bedroom, in battles over right and wrong, women like a chance to discuss what all this means, to express feelings (we will explain what those are in our next book), and to go over and over the wrong territory until you are exhausted and they believe you finally understand what they were upset about.

Go with them, guys. They don't mean any harm by this. All we can say in justification is what we have said before—if our theory is wrong, it proves the theory, since guys created it.

Of course that doesn't mean we get a free pass out of the Land of Wrong. You guys shouldn't expect one either. Just remember—try to use wrong to your advantage, but if it isn't working, it isn't working. Go with the flow.

We hope the Theory of Wrong works for you or at least doesn't hurt—because even if the theory is right, you might be wrong. Get used to it. Just like this book, wrong eventually comes to an end and you can get back to whatever it was you were doing before you looked at the beautiful entrance to the Land of Wrong and asked yourself innocently, "I wonder what's inside there?"

It was a wrong move on your part, but it's a place all guys end up in now and then. What we've done is install amenities to make your stay a little more pleasant and perhaps a little shorter.

The End

Advice for a Wrong Guy's Inner Baboon

After observing baboons in the wild for fun and enlightenment, scientist Robert Sapolsky discovered a possibly relevant point to the baboons on couches across America. Certain baboons, who asked to remain nameless, don't pursue the dominance game.

They opt out and during their mating years, they reproduce through covert mating with females who prefer them. This serves them well in old age, because they have learned to make friends with females. So, as they age they continue to make or keep friends—even though the relationships become platonic.

Meanwhile, top baboons grow old, lose their position, and are treated badly by the new dominant males, who pick on them mercilessly. Sometimes, these baboons head out in old age for other groups—leaving themselves exposed to threats until they find a new home, if they survive.

Perhaps, we wrong males can learn a lesson from the baboon, or our wives can learn a lesson about the baboon in the living room. Be friendly with women— someday, you might need one or more as a friend.

See *The Trouble with Testosterone*, "The Graying of the Troop," 1997 by Robert M. Sapolsky.

About the Authors

Jim Thielman has written articles, a biography, a novel and humor. Mixed with the occasional wit is even more occasional wisdom honed by experience as a teacher, journalist, and business communicator. Jim learned to read and translate science at a national laboratory, so in addition to the funny stories, *The Theory of Wrong* provides bite sized nuggets of the latest gender research.

If you recognize yourself or friends in *The Theory of Wrong*, it may be because Jim and Bob have collected many true stories and observations through long experience as married guys. Contact: jim@wrongtreeink.com

Bob Heck has long experience in high-level management of technical projects. Bob developed the Theory of Wrong and continues to add new material to the creative mill. Bob's creativity and drive has moved the partners forward from the seed of an idea to the reality of Wrong Tree Ink and The Theory of Wrong.

Bob also oversees the web site that connects us with the community of people who enjoy sharing stories of wrong through our newsletter, contest and future books. Bob's hope is that *The Theory of Wrong* will be right for you, your family and many of your friends. Contact: bob@wrongtreeink.com.

Why visit our web site?

Books: We offer our current book through our website, not an issue for you who are reading this, but useful should you choose to annoy someone with a gift of *The Theory of Wrong* or see if our next book is available.

Yes, someday, we will offer more books, mugs, t-shirts, cd's, tapes, videos, and wrong salt and pepper shakers (the pepper goes in the salt shaker). We also plan to create a wrong black belt made of imitation something or other.

Contest and Newsletter: Right now you can enter our wrong contest. Go to the web site and enter text of your own tale of wrong. We will pick a winner on a yet to be determined schedule—possibly once a month. Some of these stories will appear in our newsletter or even in future books.

Web site adress: www.theoryofwrong.com

Our email addresses are below:
jim@wrongtreeink.com
bob@wrongtreeink.com

Thanks for your interest in this book. Without your support, we would be wrong and unsupported, which might even be fatal for all we know.

Visit us at theoryofwrong.com. A Google search for Theory of Wrong also works.

Quick Order Form

Please send _____ copies of *The Theory of Wrong*.
I understand that I may return any of them for a full
refund—for any reason, no questions asked.

Name: _____

Address: _____

City: _____ State: ____ Zip: _____

Email Address: _____

Book price: $14.95
> Sales Tax: Add 8.3% ($1.24 per book) for books shipped
> to WA addresses. Shipping and handling: $4 for first book,
> $1.00 each for additional books ($5 for 2, etc.).

Payment:
> ❏ Check   ❏ Credit Card   ❏ Visa   ❏ MasterCard
>
> Card number: __ _____
>
> Name on card: _____
>
> Signature: _____ Exp. Date: _____

Please send more FREE information on:
> ❏ Speaking opportunities   ❏ Other books & products

BOOK ORDERS:

Fax: 509.628.3710

Phone: 509.628.9180

Online: www.theoryofwrong.com

Mail: Wrong Tree Ink, LLC
PO Box 309, Richland, WA 99352

BIN TRAVERLER FORM

Cut By: PEDRO CASTILLO #11 Qty 58 Date 07-23-26

Scanned By: _____ Qty _____ Date _____

Scanned Batch ID's

_____   _____

Notes / Exceptions

_____